This Too Shall Pass

Discovering Hope
in Seasons of Suffering

Kaitlyn C. Scott

Published by Market Refined Publishing,
An Imprint of Market Refined Media, LLC
193 Cleo Circle
Ringgold GA 30736
marketrefinedmedia.com

Cover and Interior Design by Nelly Murariu at PixBeeDesigns.com
Manuscript Edits by Kerwin Stover and Market Refined Media
Headshot taken by Janie Edwards at janieedwards.com
Family photo taken by Brittany Scheer

Print ISBN: 979-8-9855797-5-8
Digital ISBN: 979-8-9855797-6-5
Library of Congress Control Number: 2022912949

First Edition: August 2022

Dedication

To my wonderful husband, Joel, and incredible children, Jael, Harvey, Esther, and Grace: I am eternally thankful for your love. I dedicate this book first and foremost to the Lord, and secondly to you because you've never given up on me. Your lives have forever changed mine for the best.

Acknowledgements

First to the source of my strength, the lifter of my head, my joy, and my song, King Jesus. I do not know how people survive without You. I know that I surely couldn't. Thank You for walking with me through the valleys and for rejoicing with me on the mountaintops. I love You with all my heart.

To my husband, Joel. You've kept your vow wholeheartedly; to stand by my side through better or worse, through sickness and in health. Thank you for loving me when I've been vibrant, but especially when I've lost my glow. Thank you for encouraging me to never give up and standing in faith for my healing. You hold the key to my heart.

To my amazing children, Jael, Harvey, Esther, and Grace. You've made this season endurable. You bring so much joy and laughter to my life! You are compassionate and thoughtful. Your prayers for my healing and the healing of others have moved mountains. You're my heroes!

My beautiful, selfless sister, Hannah! You've been a lifeline to me in this season. Thank you for loving me and my family so well. Thank you for each day you came over and took care of us. For giving my kids baths, watching Hallmark movies with Jael while I napped, picking up groceries, praying over me, and taking care of Grace while I healed. I love you beyond measure and have never taken for granted the many ways you've laid down your life for ours.

To my mother, Katherine. I do not know what I'd do without you. Thank you for making me turkey soup for five weeks straight! Thank you for praying diligently, reminding me that this too shall pass. Thank you for being a woman of faith, and always pointing me to Jesus. I love you BMITW! The world is better because you're in it, and I'm the luckiest to be able to call you mom.

To my father, Kerwin. Thank you for being the first one to read through my book and editing it so well. Your significant role in the development of this dream is something I will treasure forever! You have a gift with words, Dad. Your tenderness shown through tears will never be forgotten. Thank you for the many times you have delivered groceries, brought over Mom's soup, done store runs for me, and so much more. I appreciate that I've never felt like an inconvenience to you. I love you very much! Your tender heart and steadfast love are something I am eternally thankful for.

To my mother-in-law, whom I prefer to call mother-in-love, Cheri. I could not have asked or prayed for a better MIL. You outshine them all! Thank you for taking care of me and the kids. Thank you for driving me to appointments, sending me encouraging texts, and always being willing to pray. I love you so much and thank God for you.

My sister, Melissa. You always lift my spirit and are filled with wisdom. I love being with you and learning how to be a better mom and wife from you. Thank you for your support and prayers throughout this season. Thank you for driving my kids and always being there for me. You are a tremendous woman who leads well in all you do.

To my other family members who have encouraged me along the way. Micah, my brother, you are always willing to help. You've encouraged me and shown me and my kids such love. Thank you. I love you! My sweet cousin, Emily, you have prayed for me and stood in faith for my healing. Thank you so very much!

I have some very powerful friends. The ones who have held my arms up during this battle include Steffani, Toni, Amanda, Emily, Harmony, Leslie, Joy, Chresa, Angie, Allie, Michelle, and many more. Thank you for loving me through the messy times, and for being faithful friends who have sought the Lord on my behalf. Thank you for fasting, praying, and believing for my healing. Everyone needs friends like you. You're the ones who would remove the tiles from a roof and lower me down to get to Jesus. From the bottom of my heart, thank you!

And to so many others who have stood in the gap praying, declaring health, and standing in faith for my miracle. I am forever thankful for you!

and through us. There are many seeds of greatness maturing inside each of us that will soon
come forth.

This is why the devil hates and fears you so
much. He knows your potential far better than
you know it yourself. He will surely attempt to
stop the seed in you from maturing and bringing
forth fruit. He will surely attempt to stop your
destiny from appearing. He will attack you from
every possible direction.

But if you stand firm in your calling, there
is absolutely nothing Satan can do to keep you
from success. Seeds of greatness are about to
explode from your life. Something that has been
growing and taking form within you for a very
long time is about to be birthed. This is true
across all cultures and nationalities. God has
rivers of living waters for all of us. So let's jump
in and swim out into the deep.

The Holy Spirit is wooing you to the deep places. He is calling you out into deep waters., where
He longs to see you do some Kingdom business.
Then, you can be sure, the wonders of God, His
miracles, His mighty power will begin to display
themselves in your life in a new way.

A Time for Asking

God's Word says something very startling:
You do not have because you do not ask.
James 4:2

Contents

Note from the Author

I pray this book encourages you and that through it you are strengthened and have greater hope for your future. If sharing my story helps even one person not give up, then it was worth writing. If that one person is you, I sincerely mean it when I say, "You were worth it." You are not alone in your suffering. And in the pain you feel, whether it be physical or emotional, know the Lord cares about you.

There were many days I wrote parts of this story while feeling ill. Chapters written through tears. Words typed as I felt like I was bouncing up and down and my body in pain. But God. He put a fire in my soul to record the truths instilled in my heart, the battle plan that will lead to victory.

Many times I felt unqualified, thinking I had to be healed first. But I believe a victorious life is one that chooses to trust God no matter what. It's from that place of victory I wrote. I felt Him leading me to start writing through the pain rather than waiting until it's gone. I hope that encourages you as well, knowing God speaks to us in every season and will use it all for our good and His glory. Our stories will not be wasted.

I wrote a song called "Just One Touch." It tells the story of the woman with the issue of blood found in Mark 5:25–34. My prayer is it will encourage and inspire those of you who need Jesus' touch on your life, and you will never stop believing for it! One touch from Him is all you need. If you'd like to listen, you can find it on iTunes, Spotify, Amazon Music, and Pandora.

Introduction

This book is for every person going through a trial, everyone in what I call a fire season. My desire in writing is to encourage hope and joy despite circumstances. Because I'm living this out right now, I feel it gives me the authority to speak to it—to speak to those of you who feel hopeless because of the pain you are enduring, or the season of waiting you are in. I'm still anticipating my miracle. But as I wait, I am seeing the goodness of God. I'm recognizing His faithfulness and not giving up. I want you to be strengthened as I have been, and together experience victory!

I know the enemy would love to take out as many people as he can, trying to convince us the best is behind us, and the future is bleak. But God! In Him our future is secure, and it is good. We must remind our souls of who we are, and what is ahead. We are the sons and daughters of the Most High God, and our inheritance is great!

Life can throw some crazy and painful curveballs, but there is a way forward because of Jesus. In Him, we can endure it all with joy! No matter what you're going through or what dream you are waiting to see unfold, you are not alone, and there is hope. Immanuel, God with us, is by your side. El Roi, the God who sees, is watching you. Heaven is cheering you on! And I am too. I want to come alongside you and share what I've been learning during a very difficult health battle. Despite daily discomfort and pain for years, I feel the strength of the Lord. And I believe He wants me to share with you what He's taught me through this journey, so you will also be strengthened.

This too shall pass, my friend. This isn't the end. Your story is not over. Don't give up on the miracle you've been contending for, and the dreams God has embedded in your heart. Rather than give up, it's time to suit up in the armor of God.

I'm going to share my story with you—the good, bad, beautiful, and overwhelming. I pray in doing so God will receive glory, and you will experience healing, hope, freedom, and joy through it. Here we go!

The Lord also will be a refuge for the oppressed, a refuge in times of trouble. And those who know Your name will put their trust in You; For You, Lord, have not forsaken those who seek You.

Psalm 9:9–10 (NKJV)

Chapter 1

What Happened

"There can be peace in the trouble,
it's the art of lifting your eyes."
- Melanie Tierce

It's been 819 days. Two years and three months of not feeling myself. I've thought about writing many times but didn't feel I had the mental strength to do so. But recently, I've felt the urge to write down the details of this story.

Have you ever been through a difficult season? One where the emotions and pain have been unbearable. Then as you came out on the other side, you forgot parts of what once made you cry. It's kind of like birthing a child, full of intensity and pain. You wonder if you have enough strength for the task. But as time passes, the pain of childbirth is forgotten.

That's why I've felt a sense to begin sharing part of my story now. Because I believe healing is coming, I want to make sure I've recorded the lessons learned through this season and the darkness I've felt. I want the light to break through so it can offer hope to others who feel lost in the shadows.

I want to have a written testimony of how God works all things for good to those who love Him and are called according to His purposes.

THE BEGINNING

So, I'll start from the beginning because it's the very best place to start. June 25th, 2019, I gave birth to my fourth child, Grace. It was a perfect, fast delivery lasting a whopping two and a half hours, with very little pain. I sensed the presence of Jesus in the room with me. I whispered His name and knew He was near. Worship music played. "Praise before my Breakthrough" by Katie Torwalt being the song heard when Grace entered the world! The first several days after having her were blissful. I had energy and felt strong following her birth.

A week postpartum I experienced some abdominal pain, so I went to use the restroom and ended up passing out. I hit my head hard enough to cause bruising. That day, my mom took me to see the midwife, I had tests run, and afterwards was cleared to go.

The next three weeks were full and fun. I hosted a 4th of July celebration, threw my sister a surprise birthday party, and enjoyed summer activities with all four of my children. My husband, Joel, headed out of town, and while he was away, on July 27th, I woke up with extreme pain caused by mastitis. I was incredibly dizzy and didn't feel safe standing with Grace. I dropped off my three older kids at the neighbors as we were scheduled to do a lemonade stand together, and then went home to lie in bed with my baby girl. My brother came over to make sure I was okay. And later my mom arrived to drive me to her house to take care of the kids and me.

We were supposed to celebrate Mom's birthday the next day and I was going to treat her to sushi. But instead, I gave her my credit card and she picked up some ready-made sushi to-go. The infection got worse as I spiked a fever, so I called my doctor and picked up a prescription.

SOMETHING CHANGED

My body went from strong and healthy, to weak and wacky. From that point on I needed help, and lots of it. I stayed with my folks until Joel got back, but once home I continued to experience on-going symptoms of dizziness, visual changes, and more (I'll get to that soon enough). Fear ran rampant in me. I was a mother of four young children who all needed my help. My oldest two were in school, which meant I had to drive them twice every weekday, as well as the extra-curricular activities they were involved in weekly. And did I mention I was working full time as the women's pastor at my church? I used up all maternity leave and some vacation days in hopes that I'd recover soon, with just a little more time. Unfortunately, that was not the case. And instead of doing what my body needed once my leave was up, I went back to working full time.

I've always been a doer. I like having things to plan and being around people. As the women's pastor, I was with ladies all the time. A group of 400-500 of us met on Wednesday mornings and evenings for a weekly Bible study. I had meetings to attend on a regular basis and was in charge of the upcoming women's conference. I felt like I couldn't put things on pause, so I pressed on. And my body cried out for me to stop!

The antibiotic I was given for mastitis messed up my stomach badly enough that I was constantly nauseated. I developed a never-ending headache that lasted five and a half months straight. I saw a gastroenterologist and was told I needed to get a colonoscopy and endoscopy.

Grace was four months old at this point and I had never been away from my babies when they were that young. But prepping for a colonoscopy is a little intense, so my sister came and picked her up for the night. I walked away from buckling up Grace in her car seat weeping. That was not what I wanted to be doing, saying goodbye to my nursing baby so I could sit on the toilet and prep to be prodded. The lower scope came back clear, but the endoscopy revealed my gut was a mess. It took the GI doctor by surprise and thus started a long process of healing for my stomach.

I'd been through stomach problems previously. From August 2016 to May 2018, I dealt with ongoing issues that finally led to the removal of my gallbladder. It took about one and a half years to heal post-surgery, and I thought that was going to be life's greatest trial. Little did I know at the time. Looking back, those couple of years pale in comparison to what I've been through recently.

I followed all the doctor's recommendations as well as home remedies I knew, like bone broth, aloe juice, and PPI's (proton pump inhibitors) specifically designed to reduce stomach acid which I had in abundance. I ate a very clean and specific diet and said goodbye to coffee. If only my stomach problems had been it. But as I mentioned, my vision had changed, and I experienced what felt like a severe, never ending tension headache. I saw a couple of neurologists, had an MRI, and was left without answers. Not having answers is hard! If you've gone through something similar and have been to numerous doctors, you know what it's like. I lived in constant pain and discomfort.

I remember a specific time at work when I sat down for coffee with a young woman in the church. I had never hated my job before, but at that moment, as my body was in pain, I wanted to escape. How could I take care of these ladies I loved when I could barely take care of myself and my children? Wednesdays were fourteen-hour workdays. When I got home and laid in bed, many times I wondered if I was going to live or if the end was near. My body was not only in pain, but it was beginning to suffer.

The women's conference had arrived, and with it came a new symptom. I began to feel like I was moving when I wasn't. My balance was off. I was the host and emcee of the event, and I remember praying, "Lord, please don't let me fall. Please don't let me pass out." I felt so off, but again, I pressed on. I looked fine on the outside, and if you didn't know I was ill, you'd have thought I was okay.

I love the quote: "Be kind, for everyone you meet is fighting a battle you know nothing about." It's easy to assume life is going well for people. Through all of this, I've learned that everyone is dealing with something. And we all need to show grace because of it.

THE RECEIVING END

I like to be on the giving end. I like being the one to cook a meal for someone in need or find a thoughtful gift to bless someone with. Unfortunately, I got so ill that I needed help with almost everything and ended up on the receiving end. That's a hard place for a giver to be.

Thank God for grocery pick-up. That service initiated at just the right time. I'd put together the grocery lists and my husband, sisters, or friends would bring the groceries home and help put them away for me. Thank God for Amazon. I'm all about supporting small businesses, but I could not go into stores because the dizziness was so bad. So, online shopping got me through Christmas.

It got to the point where friends drove my kids to school and back (thank you, Chresa, Joel, and Jess). I missed out on volunteering in Jael and Harvey's classes. My younger sister, Hannah, became a lifeline for me. I do not know what I would have done without her. I tear up as I write this. She drove to my house twice a week and took care of my kids so I could rest. She cooked our meals, cleaned the home, bathed my children (my balance got so bad that I didn't feel safe to bathe my littles, so Hannah would for me), and prayed for me all the time.

I will never forget one particular day when she prayed over me. I was lying in bed, wondering if I was dying. She came into my room and began to intercede. She battled on my behalf, unwilling to let the enemy win on her watch. As she prayed, I heard God tell me to rise up, so I did. I joined Hannah in intercession, declaring that I would live and not die!

Exodus 17:8-16 (NLT) says, *"While the people of Israel were still at Rephidim, the warriors of Amalek attacked them. Moses* commanded Joshua, 'Choose some men to go out and fight the army of Amalek for us. Tomorrow, I will stand at the top of the hill, holding the staff of God in my hand.' So Joshua did what Moses had commanded and fought the army of Amalek. Meanwhile, Moses, Aaron, and Hur climbed to the top of a nearby hill. As long as Moses held up the staff in his hand, the Israelites had the advantage. But whenever he dropped his hand, the Amalekites gained the advantage. Moses' arms soon became so tired he could no longer hold them up. So Aaron and Hur found a stone for him to sit on. Then they stood on each side of Moses, holding up his hands. So his hands held steady until sunset. As a result, Joshua overwhelmed the army of Amalek in battle. After the victory, the LORD instructed Moses, 'Write this down on a scroll as a permanent reminder, and read it aloud to Joshua: I will erase the memory of Amalek from under heaven.' Moses built an altar there and named it Yahweh-Nissi (which means "the LORD is my banner"). He said, 'They have raised their fist against the LORD's throne, so now the LORD will be at war with Amalek generation after generation.'"

As long as Moses' arms were lifted up, Israel prevailed. But his hands grew weary, and he needed help. So, Aaron and Hur stood beside him and supported him through the battle until there was victory! There are times in our lives when we need the same kind of help from those around us. We need a friend to come and watch our kids or a sister to clean our toilets. As hard as it is to receive help, sometimes God allows our circumstances to require it.

Women I pastored came to my house, brought my family meals, and prayed over me. It was incredibly humbling and oh so precious. I felt a sense of guilt because I was supposed to be the one caring for them. I wept as they thanked me for allowing them to come and minister.

I'd send a text to a group of friends on the really hard days. I'd tell them I needed some back up, that I was too weak to fight, and they'd fight for me. Almost every time I got that back up, the symptoms would lessen. Prayer works. It's powerful and brings breakthrough. There was no shame in the times I felt too weak to pray and asked others to war for me while I rested and wept. And there's no shame in asking for help when you need it too, my friend. We all walk through hard seasons and can't expect to go our entire lives without needing help. It takes humility to receive, so I encourage you to humble yourself and let others care for you when you need it.

A powerful story in the New Testament that has impacted me during this season is found in Luke 5:17–20 (NKJV). *"Now it happened on a certain day, as He was teaching, that there were Pharisees and teachers of the law sitting by, who had come out of every town of Galilee, Judea, and Jerusalem. And the power of the Lord was present to heal them. Then behold, men brought on a bed a man who was paralyzed, whom they sought to bring in and lay before Him. And when they could not find how they might bring him in, because of the crowd, they went up on the housetop and let him down with his bed through the tiling into the midst before Jesus. When He saw their faith, He said to him, 'Man, your sins are forgiven you.'"*

Then jumping to verse 24b–25, *"He said to the man who was paralyzed, 'I say to you, arise, take up your bed, and go to your house.' Immediately he rose up before them, took up what he had been lying on, and departed to his own house, glorifying God."*

The footnote about this story says, "It wasn't the paralytic's faith that impressed Jesus, but the faith of his friends. Jesus responded to their faith and healed the man."

Whoa! You might want to read that again. Jesus responded to the faith of the *friends*! Sometimes we can get so discouraged by our situation that we don't have faith to see past our pain. That's when we need the type of friends who will take tiles off a roof and lower us down in the middle of a crowd to get to Jesus, believing He is the answer. Jesus is who we need to bring life into the circumstances that cause us to almost give up.

I am surrounded by family and friends who have contended and continue to contend for my miracle. I believe it has caught the attention of Jesus and in due time, I will be healed. It makes me want to be this kind of friend to others! When I hear about someone whose marriage is falling apart, I want to be the one who declares a miracle into their union. Or when a friend loses their job, I want to stand beside them and believe for God to open the best door possible. When a friend comes to me in tears because their mom has been given a life-threatening diagnosis, I want to declare life over their body every day.

Do you feel like your faith can move mountains? Perhaps not but remember that even faith the size of a mustard seed does! And if all your faith seems lost, it's time to call on those around you. Ask them to lift up your hands and help get you to Jesus. Ask them to lower you through the roof into His presence. Let their faith carry you to Him. The Lord will encounter you there and you'll never be the same. If you don't have faith-filled friends, let's pray together for them now:

Heavenly Father,

You created us for community, and You want to surround us with friends who will walk with us through all of life's ups and downs. Right now, we pray for faith-filled friends—the type who won't stop believing for Your best in our lives. We ask You for the kind of friends who will carry us to Jesus, take the tiles off the roof and lower us right smack dab in front of You, our Savior and Healer. We're asking for kindred spirit friendships.

In Your powerful name we pray, Amen.

Do you feel like your faith can move mountains?
Perhaps not, but remember that
even faith the size of a mustard seed does!

Early on in this journey, I had to get a word from the Lord for my situation. Too many fears were swarming in my mind, and I needed something to stand on. A *rhema word* from Him (God's word spoken to me).

God spoke to me through a fellow believer, saying, "This too shall pass," and I've clung to that word ever since. Have I needed to be reminded of it by those around me? Absolutely. But in my heart, I've treasured that word and have tried to keep it safe.

What is God speaking to you? What rhema word does He want you to cling to? Guard it! Don't let it be stolen from you. Hide His word in your heart (Psalm 119:11). Perhaps you need to hear today that this too shall pass for you! This is not the end of your story. God sees it all. He sees the end from the beginning. And we have to believe, according to Romans 8:28 (NKJV), that *"all things work together for good to those who love God and are called according to His purpose."*

What we focus on, we give power to. For me to be victorious, I had to focus on the truth, or I was going to sink. Melanie Tierce's song "One More Step" has a line in it that became an anthem in my heart: "There can be peace in the trouble, it's the art of lifting your eyes."

Not only did I need a rhema word from God, but I also had to keep my eyes on Him. Remember when Peter stepped out on the water to go to Jesus? The moment he took his eyes off Him and looked onto the stormy sea, he began to sink. What if he had kept his eyes focused on the Lord the entire time? He would have been a wave walker.

Okay, let's get back to my health journey.

The October women's conference ended, and I was exhausted. I started to think about resigning, but I wasn't quite ready to make that decision.

I survived the holidays. It was the first Christmas season I didn't thoroughly love. Every tradition was difficult, yet I did them anyway. I didn't want my kids and husband adventuring off to get a tree without me, but I paid for it later. Any time I did anything extra, I paid for it. My body got weaker, I felt sicker, and I spent more time in bed and more time crying because I was in bed. It was a grievous circle.

My mother-in-law, whom I prefer to call *mother-in-love*, helped watch the kids for me twice a week. I could not have asked or prayed for a better mother-in-love, by the way. And on those days, I laid in bed and watched Hallmark movies.

Any other Hallmark lovers out there? I didn't want to watch anything with an unknown or sad ending. Nothing suspenseful or stressful. So Hallmark was my *go-to*. I watched hours upon hours of the same storyline and the inevitable brush of the face. You know, when the guy who will end up with the girl wipes chocolate, or flour, or dust off her face? I don't think it's a legit Hallmark movie without a face wipe. But I digress.

Now, that might sound pretty awesome to some of you (or a nightmare if you're like my husband and can't stand Hallmarks) but it's one thing to choose to lie in bed and watch movies. It's another to feel forced into it.

IT WAS TIME

By late January I'd go to work feeling completely ill every day. I had to sit when I talked with people. I'd hold my head in my hands because it was in constant pain. I was continually wincing my eyes because they hurt so badly. One of the precious women I served with, dear Linda, said to me one day, "Kaitlyn, you look like you're suffering." I told her she was right. I began to cry and express my decision it was time for me to resign. She prayed over me and agreed.

I worked with one of my dearest friends on this planet, Steffani. We pastored together. We talk about everything. We laugh and cry together. I didn't want to leave her or the hundreds of beautiful women my heart had grown to love so deeply, but it was time. I did not have a choice. My body could not handle the workload any longer.

The day I said goodbye to the ladies, Steffani had to help hold me up. My body was too weak to stand alone. The women brought me flowers because flowers are my favorite. I went home with so many of them that you could have mistaken my house for a nursery. It was wonderful! Steffani drove me home and I remember feeling so weak that I went straight to my bed. Saying goodbye was not easy. I still grieve what once was, but it's ok. God knows, and in His timing I'll minister again. (I miss you, ladies, and I love you oh so much.)

Before my position in women's ministry, I led worship. My husband and I were worship pastors together. I'd been involved in ministry from the time I was in sixth grade. I never imagined having to take a break from it. But here I am... still!

Thankfully, my identity hasn't been wrapped up in what I do. I loved my job so much, and I loved the people more. But before the title of worship pastor or women's pastor, I'd just been Kaitlyn— a child of God, loved by Him and my family.

I'm a wife and a mother. I've often told my children the absolute best job in the world is being their mom, and I've meant it. I wanted a season at home with them. I didn't want it under these circumstances but being home with them every day is something I will never regret. I'm homeschooling them now and I love it. I planted more flowers and am planning for a garden next spring. Dreams in my heart are coming true in the midst of suffering. I may not be in active ministry within a church, but I am feeling God's goodness during this challenging season. I'll say more about this later.

THE LIST

Many people said I'd get better quickly after resigning. I thought so too, but that wasn't the case. In fact, things got much worse. I saw various doctors including our family physician, who referred me to the Mayo Clinic. I was, however, declined at the time. I went through the following to try to figure out what was going on in my body, desperate to get better:

* I saw a functional doctor (focuses on identifying the root cause of disease).
* I went to a homeopathic doctor (focuses on helping you get healthy and stay healthy through natural sources).
* I saw an Atlas chiropractor 32 times.
* I tried physical therapy with a couple of different PT's.
* I had muscle activation therapy.
* I did vestibular therapy (helps alleviate symptoms caused by vestibular problems).
* I tried acupuncture.
* I did ozone therapy (look this up if interested).
* I lay on an infrared bed (look up the purpose if interested).
* I spent thousands of dollars on IV's. (As a side note, when I got IV's of NAD [Nicotinamide Adenine Dinucleotide], which is an intravenous treatment that strengthens your cells by stimulating cell regeneration, it did help decrease nerve pain. If you or someone you know has nerve pain, I'd suggest trying it.)
* I saw a connective tissue specialist.
* I went to a cranial sacral doctor who said she didn't know how I was alive based on my cranial structure being so out of alignment.
* I saw a Doctor of Physical Therapy who does specialized testing for intracranial hypertension and cerebral spinal fluid leaks.

* I went to four different ENT's and tested for manière's disease and inner ear nerve issues. ... I saw another neurologist and had another MRI.
* I went to an eye doctor.
* I had dental work done to see if it was the cause of any underlying issues.
* I went to a maxillofacial surgeon.
* I took supplements to help with the healing of my nerves and to better support my immune system, as well as 1,500 mgs of Gabapentin and 60 mgs of Duloxetine daily.

The medications helped with the nerve pain, but it meant I was incredibly medicated morning, noon, and night, and therefore quite tired all the time. I needed help to function because before the meds, nerve pain had increased exponentially. My face was so tender that when my kids touched it, I'd wince. It hurt to brush my hair. I didn't blow it dry for many months. It was hard to take a shower. Washing my face was so painful and baths became difficult too, because I felt like I was bobbing up and down all the time. Everything became a struggle.

I wound up with cellulitis, a skin infection, in both of my ears. This bacterium leaked a foul discharge and got into little scrapes in my ears. Gross, I know. And in the middle of the night, on March 18th, two days before my 35th birthday, Joel took me to the ER. I had cauliflower ears and was having a hard time hearing. At the hospital, I was given intravenous antibiotics so the infection wouldn't spread. I spiked a high fever the meds didn't bring down but was eventually sent home. It was a bizarre reaction that the doctors had never seen before.

Through it all, Joel was a great caretaker. He had to assist me in walking and holding me up to use the restroom. He gave me antibiotics when I was supposed to take them and made sure I stayed hydrated. What a guy. When we said our vows, we meant them: through better or worse, in sickness and in health.

After that ER visit, I became debilitated. I couldn't clean. I felt safest just lying down. I was in bed the second I said goodnight to the kids, relieved the day was over. And I dreaded the sunrise that would inevitably come. I did not feel like I was living. I was simply surviving, crying out to God for a miracle. Why me? Why this? What did I do? The questions, the sorrow, the grief of what felt taken from me. It was overwhelming.

I had to stop nursing Gracie. I still tear up thinking about it. The medications I was taking weren't safe for her system. That was a hard pill to swallow (pun intended). It was time for 24/7 help, so I went to my parents' house with the kids.

THE LOVE OF FAMILY

Let me take a moment to tell you about my mom. Her name is Katherine, and she's one of the most selfless, thoughtful, support-ive people you'll ever meet. She gave up their master bedroom and had it made over for me. She bought a TV for the room so that I'd be able to watch Hallmarks. She took in me and my children for almost five weeks, making sure I always had turkey soup on hand. My legs were in constant pain, so she'd rub them for hours to help bring a little relief. She helped my kids with school. She fed them, bathed them, and loved us all so well.

My sister Hannah set up a playpen in her room for Gracie to sleep in so that she could get up with her in the night instead of me. Hannah became like a second momma to her. Their bond is so special, and I'm overwhelmingly thankful for it.

During the five weeks spent at my parents' house, I experi-enced some of the darkest moments in this journey.

My body went through the most intense symptoms of the entire two plus years while I was there. My head was so full of pres-sure it felt like it would pop. I couldn't sleep because I was in too much pain. My nerves kept me awake, sending shooting signals throughout my body. My jaw wouldn't stay shut, so I had to lay with pillows propped up around my face to hold it still. I couldn't stand up for long. Everything that brought me comfort felt stripped away... baths, coffee, sleep. I was in constant agony. There were many times I'd turn on the TV in the middle of the night because I wasn't sleeping, and I needed some form of distraction.

Joel bought me a great speaker so that I could fill the room with worship music. My go-to album was Steffany Gretzinger's *Forever Amen*. The song "No One Ever Cared for Me Like Jesus" was so very comforting. It was hard to read, so reading the Bible was put on hold for a while. Instead, I listened to healing scriptures and had a Songs of Victory playlist.

MY PLAYLIST

These are the songs I've listened to on repeat, in case you need a victory playlist too:

* "Raise a Hallelujah" (Live) by Bethel Music
* "Victory is Yours" (Live) by Bethel Music
* "See A Victory" by Elevation Worship
* "Surrounded (Fight My Battles)" by UPPERROOM
* "Fight for Me" by Dustin Smith
* "Goodness of God" (Live) by Bethel Music
* "Remember" by Bryan and Katie Torwalt
* "Way Maker" (Live) by Leeland
* "I Speak Jesus" by Here Be Lions
* "This is a Move" (live) by Brandon Lake
* "Praise Before My Breakthrough" by Bryan and Katie Torwalt
* "Breakthrough" (Live) by The Belonging Co
* "Promises" by Maverick City Music
* "Freedom is Coming" by Bryan and Katie Torwalt
* "Gratitude" by Brandon Lake
* "House of Miracles" by Brandon Lake

* "Too Good to Not Believe" by Bethel Music, Brandon Lake
* "Miracle in the Works" by Bryan and Katie Torwalt
* "Healing Scriptures and Bible Verses" by Heather Hair
* "You Came (Lazarus)" by Bethel Music

When the time came for me to go home, I felt scared, knowing there was still so much healing that needed to happen. But I'd gotten through the darkest nights. I made it through every hard day. And I had to continue to rely on the Lord for His strength to see me through!

For in You, O Lord, I hope;
You will hear, O Lord my God.
Psalm 38:15 (NKJV)

Chapter 2

God Is with Us

*"Fear not, for I have redeemed you; I have called you by
your name, you are mine. When you pass through the
waters, I will be with you; and through the rivers, they shall
not overwhelm you; when you walk through fire, you shall
not be burned, and the flame shall not consume you."*
Isaiah 43:1b-2 (ESV)

When we're in a trial, it's the strength of the Lord that will walk us through it. And He *will* get us through it. David said, *"Though I walk through the valley of the shadow of death"* (Psalm 23:4 ESV). Though I walk through. He didn't say, "Though I *stay* in the valley of the shadow of death." We will get through the difficult seasons. And while we are walking through them, we don't have to fear any evil, because He is with us! He is Immanuel, God with us.

WITH US IN THE FIRE

I'm reminded of the story of Shadrach, Meshach, and Abed-Nego. They would not worship King Nebuchadnezzar's gods or the golden image they were commanded to bow down to. So, King Neb threw them into a fiery furnace. He had it heated seven times hotter than normal. It was so hot that the flames killed the men who brought Shadrach, Meshach, and Abed-Nego to it. I love how the three of them responded to the king when they heard that they'd be thrown in the furnace.

Daniel 3:16-18 (NKJV) says, "*Shadrach, Meshach, and Abed-Nego answered and said to the king, 'O Nebuchadnezzar, we have no need to answer you in this matter. If that is the case, our God whom we serve is able to deliver us from the burning fiery furnace, and He will deliver us from your hand, O king. But if not, let it be known to you, O king, that we do not serve your gods, nor will we worship the gold image which you have set up.'*"

What happened next? They were cast into the fiery furnace. But God!

"*'Look!' he answered, 'I see four men loose, walking in the midst of the fire; and they are not hurt, and the form of the fourth is like the Son of God.' Then Nebuchadnezzar went near the mouth of the burning fiery furnace and spoke, saying, 'Shadrach, Meshach, and Abed-Nego, servants of the Most High God, come out, and come here.' Then Shadrach, Meshach, and Abed-Nego came from the midst of the fire. And the satraps, administrators, governors, and the king's counselors gathered together, and they saw these men on whose bodies the fire had no power; the hair of their head was not singed nor were their garments affected, and the smell of fire was not on them. Nebuchadnezzar spoke, saying, 'Blessed be the God of Shadrach, Meshach, and Abed-Nego, who sent His Angel and delivered His servants who trusted in Him, and they have frustrated the king's word, and yielded their bodies, that they should not serve nor worship any god except their own God!'*" (Daniel 3:25-28 NKJV)

Come on! If that doesn't encourage you, I don't know what will! These men were put into a blazing hot furnace, but the FIRE

HAD NO POWER over them, and THEY DIDN'T EVEN SMELL LIKE SMOKE. God is with us in the fire. He sends help. He protects. And as we honor Him, we come out of those Job-like seasons unharmed. Even more, the smell of smoke from the fire we've encountered won't even be present on us. That's what I want! When this is all over, I don't want to smell like smoke. I want to smell like a sweet fragrant offering to the Lord!

WITH US IN THE STORM

God is not only with us in the fire, but He is also with us in the storm. I love the story of Jesus asleep on the boat as the storm raged. It's found in Matthew 8:23-27 (NIV). *"Then he got into the boat and his disciples followed him. Suddenly a furious storm came up on the lake, so that the waves swept over the boat. But Jesus was sleeping. The disciples went and woke him, saying, 'Lord, save us! We're going to drown!' He replied, 'You of little faith, why are you so afraid?' Then he got up and rebuked the winds and the waves, and it was completely calm. The men were amazed and asked, 'What kind of man is this? Even the winds and the waves obey Him!'"*

When we're in the middle of a storm, we might believe Jesus is with us but doubt He is aware of everything going on around us. Like the disciples, we cry out, "Jesus! Save me! I'm not going to make it if you don't wake up!" And Jesus responds, "Why are you so afraid?" Jesus was with them in that boat. The disciples had seen Him perform miracle after miracle, and yet the storm caused them to fear for their lives. How might the disciples have responded in a better way in that situation? They should have followed Jesus' example, and chosen to rest, knowing He was with them. And if He was sleeping through the storm, they could too.

The storm caused them to forget about the power that was with them. I've been guilty of the same thing. I know God is with me, but in moments that feel overwhelming, I've given into fear instead of following Jesus' example and choosing peace and rest. Lord, forgive me.

---

*Don't let the storm around you cause
you to forget about the power that is with you.*

Because of the various and oftentimes scary symptoms my body has gone through, I've had to learn how to speak to fear. How to rise above it. How to remind myself of the truths I know. What does this look like? Many nights, as I've been in bed, I've quoted Scripture. I've reminded my soul of the faithfulness of God. That He is with me and won't let me die before my time. On harder days, I tell myself that better ones will come again.

I've taken deep breaths, listened to worship music, and prayed in the spirit. Praying in the Spirit (speaking in tongues) is a gift, and something we should be doing every day! Jude 1:20 and 1 Corinthians 14:4 tells us it builds us up. It's a sign that should accompany those who believe (Mark 16:17). And when we don't know what to pray, the Spirit in us does (Romans 8:26–27)! It strengthens our inner man and is truly a gift from God to us.

If you have your prayer language, I'd encourage you to use it daily! If you don't have it, know that it's a gift available to those who have received Jesus as their Lord and Savior. Ask Him for it. And if you need more help or would like further direction, please reach out to me or someone else who would love to help you!

THE ANCHOR

Through this season, I've needed an anchor to keep me grounded. And that anchor is hope (Hebrews 6:19). What is the definition of hope? It is expectation. Oftentimes in the Bible, it's joyful expectation and anticipation of good. God wants us to live with an expectation and joyful anticipation of good things to come. We are to live taking hold of the hope we have in the promises of God. And when we do, we will be secured and able to endure the stormy seasons.

Romans 15:13 (NIV) says, *"May the God of hope fill you with all joy and peace as you trust in him, so that you may overflow with hope by the power of the Holy Spirit."* It is possible to overflow with hope, as we trust in Him. Wow! Are you overflowing with hope right now? Are you joyfully expecting good things to come? Are you expecting your situation to turn around? This is the kind of hope God wants us to walk in—the kind that fully trusts His ability to bring about good, no matter the circumstances.

Some days I feel like I will never be normal again. Those are the days I weep the most. The days I have hope that this too shall pass, are the ones I manage to get through with the strength of the Lord. We need hope in our lives. And to have it, we must trust the Lord.

I like what Bill and Beni Johnson wrote in their devotional "Peace in Every Storm." "If we find ourselves sinking into hopelessness, we are falling into the lie of believing that there are certain things outside of God's reach."

Hope strengthens us. Isaiah 40:31 (NIV) says, *"But those who hope in the LORD will renew their strength. They will soar on wings like eagles; they will run and not grow weary, they will walk and not be faint."*

Faith is developed in us when we live with hope. Hebrews 11:1 (NKJV) says, *"Now faith is the substance of things hoped for, the evidence of things not seen."*

I love Hebrews 11:11 because we see that Sarah received both faith and strength when she had hope in the promise God gave her—the promise to bear a son in her old age (90 years old). Hebrews 11:11 (NKJV) says, *"By faith Sarah herself also received strength to conceive seed, and she bore a child when she was past the age, because she judged Him faithful who had promised."*

Sarah had hope in the promises of God. And through her faith in Him, she received strength which led to a miracle!

But she didn't immediately respond in faith when God told her she would have a baby of her own. Let's dig into the story. It's found in Genesis 18:9–14a (NIV).

Three visitors came near Abraham's tent, and he hosted them well, providing refreshments. They had a word from the Lord for him. *"'Where is your wife Sarah?' they asked him. 'There, in the tent,' he said. Then one of them said, 'I will surely return to you about this time next year, and Sarah your wife will have a son.' Now Sarah was listening at the entrance to the tent, which was behind him. Abraham and Sarah were already very old, and Sarah was past the age of childbearing. So Sarah laughed to herself as she thought, 'After I am worn out and my lord is old, will I now have this pleasure?' Then the Lord said to Abraham, 'Why did Sarah laugh and say, 'Will I really have a child, now that I am old?' Is anything too hard for the Lord?'"*

Is there anything too hard for the Lord? Do you have a prodigal son or daughter? Maybe your marriage looks hopeless, or you've received a terrible medical diagnosis. Maybe your finances are a wreck. What looks impossible in your life? For Sarah, it was her age. She was well-past the age of childbearing. In the natural, it should not have happened... BUT GOD. (This is a side note, but anytime I see the words *but God* in the Word, I highlight them. I love *but God* stories!)

Continuing with Genesis 18:14b–15 (NIV), *"'I will return to you at the appointed time next year, and Sarah will have a son.' Sarah was afraid, so she lied and said, 'I did not laugh.' But he said, 'Yes, you did laugh.'"*

The word *laugh* in this passage is the Hebrew word *tsachaq*, which means to laugh outright, mock, play, and make sport.

A few chapters later in Genesis 21:1-3, 5-7 (NKJV) we read, *"And the Lord visited Sarah as He had said, and the Lord did for Sarah as He had spoken."* The word *spoken* here is the word *dabar* which means to speak, say, promise, pronounce. *"For Sarah conceived and bore Abraham a son in his old age, at the set time of which God had spoken to him. And Abraham called the name of his son who was born to him—whom Sarah bore to him—Isaac.*

Now Abraham was one hundred years old when his son Isaac was born to him. And Sarah said, 'God has made me laugh, and all who hear will laugh with me.' She also said, 'Who would have said to Abraham that Sarah would nurse children? For I have borne him a son in his old age.'"

I like reading verses 6-7 in The Message version too. "*Sarah said, 'God has blessed me with laughter and all who get the news will laugh with me!' She also said, 'Whoever would have suggested to Abraham that Sarah would one day nurse a baby! Yet here I am! I've given the old man a son!'"*

Sarah laughed two times. At first, she laughed in doubt and mockery at the word of the Lord that she would conceive. However, something happened from the point of her doubting to her conceiving. As we read earlier in Hebrews 11:11, by faith Sarah herself received strength to conceive seed, and she bore a child when she was past the age, because she judged Him faithful who had promised.

She is the first woman listed in the Hall of Faith in Hebrews 11. After she received the word, faith must have stirred up in her. She took hold of the word of the Lord, and faith gave her the strength to conceive and carry God's promise. Her laughter that started as doubt, ended in rejoicing. It went from "Ha, ha, yea right," to "He will do it!" I love this!

They even named their son Isaac, which translates to *he laughs*. Sarah's pregnancy and Isaac's birth caused a lot of laughter!

God wants more laughter in your life too. He wants to take your doubt that's causing you to question His ability to come through for you, and plant a word in your heart that takes root. He wants that firmly rooted word to then increase your faith so much that you will be able to declare God faithful. That you'll believe His every promise, no matter how impossible it might seem. Once you see that promise come to pass, you'll laugh, and others will laugh with you, rejoicing in God's faithfulness! Won't He do it!?

Let's choose to be faith-filled, unshakable and secure in the Lord. This comes through trusting in the goodness and faithfulness of God. Jeremiah 17:7-8 (ESV) says, *"Blessed is the man who trusts in the Lord, whose trust is the Lord. He is like a tree planted by water, that sends out its roots by the stream, and does not fear when heat comes, for its leaves remain green, and is not anxious in the year of drought, for it does not cease to bear fruit."*

WITH US IN THE WIND

If you're like me, you're not a big fan of wind. A gentle breeze is great, but a forceful wind? No, thanks. However, my perspective changed when I read about a desert experiment where a biodome with a controlled environment had everything needed for trees, vegetables, and fruits to grow. The hope was that providing the right soil, filtered light, and purified air and water would make the best living environment, not only for the plants but also for humans.

For a while, people lived there, and everything seemed to thrive until the trees reached a certain height and fell over. The scientists were confused. Then it dawned on them they'd forgotten to add the element of wind.

Trees need wind for their roots to grow deep. Without wind blowing against them, their roots are shallow, which in turn keeps the trees weak and unable to continue growing. (To learn more, visit NaturalAwakenings.com for the article titled "Strong Winds Strong Roots: What Trees Teach Us About Life" by Dennis Merrit.)

Just as wind helps the roots of trees grow deeper and stronger, when we encounter *wind* in life, it's an opportunity for us to grow in our walk with God. Sounds nice, doesn't it: growing in our walk with God? But that's easier said than done, isn't it?

How do we learn to appreciate the wind? About a month after I heard the biodome story, I woke up in the night due to a crazy storm. At first, I was frustrated. But my perspective changed as I remembered trees needed wind for their roots to be strengthened. With each gust, the trees were growing stronger. It made me appreciate what the wind was doing for their roots.

Most of us would much rather walk through life never having to go through a storm. When we face a trial, our prayer often goes something like this: "God please fix this now! Take away my pain, heal my body! Make this stop!" And too often, we doubt God's faithfulness. But we must know God is with us through it all. He has a plan, and it is good. He allows the storms, but we can rest in Him through them, knowing He will bring a calm to them in time. Storms don't last forever.

If you're experiencing the frustration of wind right now, know that even if you don't feel it, God is strengthening you in Him. The wind will die down. This too shall pass. You will come through this season because God is with you!

"Hold on to the rope of hope." God clearly spoke that to my heart during this battle. Months later, my ten-year-old daughter, Jael, told me God gave her a picture of me dangling on the edge of a cliff. I was holding on to a rope, and I was scared to fall. But eventually that rope pulled me up to solid ground. She felt like God was showing her that one day I will be healed. And although it can be scary now, that rope will get me to a firm foundation. WOW! The prophetic picture that God gave to her confirmed the rhema word He had spoken to me.

I share this with you to encourage you to do the same. Hold tightly to the rope of hope, fiercely determined to not let go. It will eventually pull you up to solid ground too.

Hold on to the rope of hope.

The Lord is my shepherd;
I shall not want.
He makes me to lie down in green pastures;
He leads me beside the still waters.
He restores my soul.
Psalm 23:1-3a (NKJV)

Chapter 3

A Higher Perspective

"For our light affliction, which is but for a moment,
is working for us a far more exceeding and eternal
weight of glory, while we do not look at the things
which are seen, but at the things which are not seen.
For the things which are seen are temporary, but
the things which are not seen are eternal."
2 Corinthians 4:17-18 (NKJV)

In Lysa Terkeurst's Bible study, *It's Not Supposed to be this Way*, she asks, "Being completely honest with yourself, are you more interested in the pain going away or in being made more like Christ?" In all honesty, my heart wants to be made more like Christ, but my prayer in times of pain is, "Please just make it go away, God." I need my mind renewed to have heaven's perspective. To know and to see what God is doing through the storms and trials of life. Perspective is *key* to overcoming.

Isaiah 55:8-9 (NIV) says, "'For my thoughts are not your thoughts, neither are your ways my ways,'" declares the Lord. 'As the heavens are higher than the earth, so are my ways higher than your ways* *and my thoughts than your thoughts.'"* God's ways and His thoughts are so much better and so much higher than ours. His perspective is perfect. His desire is for us to connect with Him, understand His heart, hear His voice, and know His Word so that the way we think and the way we live begin to conform and come into alignment with His thoughts and His ways. God sees the big picture when we only see in part. How often do we look back and say, "Oh... now I understand, Lord. Now I see how you worked in that situation." But in the moment, it's easy to question and doubt, isn't it?

The story of the Israelites in Exodus and Numbers is a good example of people who experienced God's faithfulness. Time and time again they took their eyes off Him and put them onto their fears or what they thought was lacking.

The Israelites were delivered out of Egypt, out of bondage and captivity, led through the Red Sea, fed manna and quail from heaven, led by a pillar of cloud by day and a pillar of fire by night, given water from a rock, and on and on and on. Yet they continually doubted God's faithfulness to them. God knew the end from the beginning, and He was leading them to their Promised Land. But in their humanity, they kept forgetting what they knew to be true about God's character. They kept forgetting the ways He'd been faithful to them, causing them to lose heaven's perspective!

I used to read this story and get so frustrated by the Israelites. *Again? You're doubting God again? You're worshiping an idol rather than the one true God? You're complaining and questioning God's goodness to you after He's been so faithful and shown Himself in miraculous ways?* But aren't we all guilty of the same things?

I have more compassion for the Israelites now because I've experienced the test of trusting God completely and I have doubted His timing like they did. God says, "Trust me," and I do for a while, until I feel like it's taking too long in the wilderness. It's been windy and I'm tired of my hair being a mess.

We have to know the character and love of God and remind ourselves of it. When God says no to something in our lives, it's because He has a better *yes*. When He says, "Wait, it's not time yet," our response needs to be trust. And when He leads us to something, we must believe He will be faithful to lead us through it.

Here are some ways to help us develop a higher perspective.

REMEMBER GOD'S FAITHFULNESS

During one intense night, I asked God what I was supposed to do. He told me to *remember*. To remind myself of who He is and what He's done. He's healed me before; He will heal me again. Over twenty years ago God miraculously and instantly healed me of hyperthyroidism. I would have been on medication for the rest of my life, but in a moment of prayer, God healed me. I've had to remind myself of this testimony time and time again. And when I do, I have hope for my current health situation.

Numbers 23:19 (NIV) says, *"God is not human, that he should lie, not a human being, that he should change his mind. Does he speak and then not act? Does he promise and not fulfill?"* God will do what He says! It's our job to remember His word and live with the expectation (hope) that it will come to pass.

The other day my five-year-old asked me if there's anything that God *can't* do. What an amazing question. I thought about it for a moment and answered, "He can't lie." When He makes a promise, He keeps it. My former pastor, John Stocker, used to say, "If God said it, I believe it, and that settles it."

Deuteronomy 4:9 (NIV) says, *"Only be careful, and watch yourselves closely so that you do not forget the things your eyes have seen or let them fade from your heart as long as you live. Teach them to your children and to their children after them."* DO NOT FORGET the things God has done! Life is not always going to make sense, but when we know who God is and recall His goodness, we will see not through the filter of disappointment, but through hope. We can then say things such as, "I don't understand Lord, but I know Your Word says You will never leave me nor forsake me. I don't feel good, God, but I know You are with me and that Your rod and Your staff comfort me."

Lamentations 3:21-23 (NKJV) says, *"This I recall to my mind, Therefore I have hope. Through the LORD's mercies we are not consumed, Because His compassions fail not. They are new every morning; Great is Your faithfulness."* When we remember who God is, what He has done, and what He has said He will do, we are filled with hope and our perspective is higher!

LIVE WITH ETERNITY IN MIND

Every trial we face and everything we go through in life is short in comparison to eternity.

2 Corinthians 4:17-18 (NKJV) says, *"For our light affliction, which is but for a moment, is working for us a far more exceeding and eternal weight of glory, while we do not look at the things which are seen, but at the things which are not seen. For the things which are seen are temporary, but the things which are not seen are eternal."*

Years ago, I was heading to the mountains to lead worship at a women's conference. I had to take Joel's diesel truck, which was on empty. He reminded me multiple times to make sure to fill it up with diesel, not regular gasoline.

As I drove to the gas station, I said to myself out loud, "Diesel, diesel, diesel, diesel, diesel." I filled up his truck and drove for about an hour before it started making a pretty distinct and unfamiliar sound. It also started to jerk, as if it was struggling to go uphill. I called Joel, worried I might have out of habit put gasoline in, instead of diesel. Joel assured me the truck wouldn't have made it that far if I had. But still, I had a gut-wrenching feeling I had made a mistake and feared I'd ruined his engine.

I made it to the conference location, called the gas station, and asked if they could tell me if I had purchased gas or diesel. They confirmed my fear. I had, in fact, filled up the diesel engine of a truck with regular gasoline.

In tears, I called Joel back. I felt terrible. I asked him what he thought would happen and he said, "Well, my truck is probably ruined." Then I lost it... bawling my head off in the parking lot of the YMCA. Joel said, "It will be okay, honey. We still have a van. We have two beautiful children. It could be worse." His kindness made me cry even more! In a way, I wanted him to yell at me because that's what I felt I deserved.

When we hung up, I sat in the truck weeping.

When we focus on that which is *temporary* versus what is *eternal*, we lose perspective. But when we place value on the eternal, our viewpoint is higher. Joel's perspective was healthy; mine was not. We still had a van, and so many reasons to give thanks. We would figure it out. In reality it wasn't that big of a deal, but I was so worried about the present situation it was hard for me to see past that moment.

It's important we remind ourselves that this life on earth is not the end. God allowed Jesus, His Son, to endure the cross and die for us. But that was not the end either! His glorious resurrection took place just three days later. And because of what Jesus suffered and endured, the greatest trial anyone has ever walked through, we have heaven to look forward to!

After the conference, we had Joel's truck towed to a nearby mechanic. He drained out every ounce of gasoline (about $90 worth) and to everyone's surprise, the truck still ran. In fact, it's been six years and is still running today! So, maybe diesel trucks really can run on gasoline! *(wink-wink)*

KEEP YOUR EYES ON JESUS

I shared the story of Peter walking on water earlier, but I think it's worth mentioning again here. It's found in Matthew 14.

Jesus and the disciples had been ministering and feeding the 5,000. Then Jesus sent the disciples ahead of Him in a boat while

He dismissed the crowd and headed to the mountainside to pray. Matthew 14:24–31 (MSG) says, *"Meanwhile, the boat was far out to sea when the wind came up against them and they were battered by the waves. At about four o'clock in the morning, Jesus came toward them walking on the water. They were scared to death. 'A ghost!' they said, crying out in terror. But Jesus was quick to comfort them. 'Courage, it's me. Don't be afraid.' Peter, suddenly bold, said, 'Master, if it's really you, call me to come to you on the water.' He said, 'Come ahead.' Jumping out of the boat, Peter walked on the water to Jesus. But when he looked down at the waves churning beneath his feet, he lost his nerve and started to sink. He cried, 'Master, save me!' Jesus didn't hesitate. He reached down and grabbed his hand. Then he said, 'Faint-heart, what got into you?'"*

When Peter was looking at Jesus, he had courage despite the storm. He had courage to get out of the boat and walk on water. *But*, when he looked at the storm around him, when he took his eyes off Jesus, that's when he began to fear and started to sink.

So many things going on in the world try to capture our attention, steal our peace, and take our focus off Jesus and onto something else. We can waste a ton of time being distracted *or*, we can turn our eyes upon Jesus to get His heart and perspective.

I've been guilty of looking at the storms and losing sight of Jesus in them. It never makes me feel better when I do. But when I look to Him, get into His Word, spend time in prayer, turn on worship, and remind my soul (my mind, will, and emotions) of who He is, courage begins to rise up in me. That's when I feel hope anchoring my soul and I begin to look different from those who are without hope.

JESUS DID IT RIGHT

Hebrews 12:1–2 (NKJV) says, *"Therefore we also, since we are surrounded by so great a cloud of witnesses, let us lay aside every weight, and the sin which so easily ensnares us, and let us run with endurance the race that is set before us, looking unto Jesus, the author and finisher of our faith, who for the joy that was set before Him endured the cross, despising the shame, and has sat down at the right hand of the throne of God."*

Let's also read Hebrews 12:2–3 in The Message version. *"Keep your eyes on Jesus, who both began and finished this race we're in. Study how he did it. Because he never lost sight of where he was headed—that exhilarating finish in and with God—he could put up with anything along the way: Cross, shame, whatever. And now he's there, in the place of honor, right alongside God. When you find yourselves flagging in your faith, go over that story again, item by item, that long litany of hostility he plowed through. That will shoot adrenaline into your souls!"*

Jesus never lost sight of God's will. He was focused and did not get tripped up by sin, fear, or even death. In His moment of agony in the Garden of Gethsemane, He asked if it was possible for God to take it from Him so He didn't have to go through this. *Yet* His response was, "Not my will, but Yours be done." He kept His focus on His Father and His Father's will. He knew God's love for Him and trusted it. Friend, we must keep our eyes on Jesus if we are to make it through life victoriously and have a higher perspective!

REMEMBER YOUR LEGACY

Why should we care about having a higher perspective? Yes, we'll be able to better endure the struggles and storms of life when we do. But the way we live will also impact others as well. It impacts our children and our children's children. It affects those around us.

Proverbs 20:7 (NKJV) says, *"The righteous man walks in his integrity; His children are blessed after him."*

Little do we know our impact and our legacy, even to the fourteenth generation! Matthew 1:17 (MSG) says, *"There were fourteen generations from Abraham to David, another fourteen from David to the Babylonian exile, and yet another fourteen from the Babylonian exile to Christ."*

Think about it for a moment. What do you want your legacy to be? Are you living it now? This will help your perspective. When you can see beyond yourself and to the future, you become aware of what you are doing to help shape it by how you are choosing to live your life now. The way you are choosing to trust God and the way you are walking through life's trials matters greatly.

Proverbs 20:7 in The Message says, *"God-loyal people, living honest lives, make it much easier for their children."*

Are we living our lives in a way that will make it easier for our children, for the next generation?

Deuteronomy 12:28 (NKJV) says, *"Observe and obey all these words which I command you, that it may go well with you and your children after you forever, when you do what is good and right in the sight of the Lord your God."*

Blessing comes through our obedience to the Lord!

I'm blessed with incredible parents. I've seen them go through many trials. Twenty years ago, they lost a son during my mom's eighth month of pregnancy. The way they responded to that time of suffering impacted my life greatly. Their ability to keep their eyes on Jesus in the midst of the storm had a lasting effect on me, probably more than they ever realized. When they found out that Justice had passed away in the womb, they came home from the doctor's visit without telling us what had happened. My mom repeated over and over again, "Kids, God is good. God is good! God is good!"

I watched my dad during worship at church in the weeks and months to follow. His arms were stretched high in praise. I can still picture it now, and I tear up as I write this. My parents taught me to draw closer to Jesus during a trial, rather than walk away from Him. Their perspective made a difference in my life. Your choices and the way you view times of trial will make a difference in those around you. Whether you're a parent or not, people are watching you. They are learning from you. You're creating a legacy *now*.

I didn't grow up rich when it comes to material possessions. We were not wealthy by any means, although I never lacked. But I have been given so much because my parents love and serve the Lord. They've lived their life to honor Him. They have lived with a higher perspective. They've remembered God's faithfulness and shared it with their children. They have kept their eyes on Jesus, and have lived with eternity in mind, and because of it, their legacy is great!

Psalm 77:11–15 (NIV) says, *"I will remember the deeds of the Lord; yes, I will remember your miracles of long ago. I will consider all your works and meditate on all your mighty deeds. Your ways, God, are holy. What god is as great as our God? You are the God who performs miracles; you display your power among the peoples. With your mighty arm you redeemed your people, the descendants of Jacob and Joseph."*

This is the God we are to keep our eyes on. A miracle working God, full of power and love. A redeeming God. A great God! As we fix our eyes on Him, the things of earth—the storms, the wind, and trials of life—will grow strangely dim in the light of His glory and grace. "Turn Your Eyes Upon Jesus" is a beautiful song, isn't it? As we do this, our roots will grow deep in Christ, and we will not be shaken.

O Lord my God, I cried out to you,
And You healed me.
Psalm 30:2 (NKJV)

Chapter 4

Our Miracle Home

"Trust in the Lord and do good; Dwell in the land and feed on His faithfulness. Delight yourself also in the Lord, and He shall give you the desires of your heart. Commit your way to the Lord, trust also in Him, and He shall bring it to pass. He shall bring forth your righteousness as the light, and your justice as the noonday."
Psalm 37:3-6 (NKJV)

Did you ever wish for something as a child? Of course you did! Maybe it was to own a horse one day, or to travel the world. Perhaps you wanted to grow up to be a princess or a firefighter. I wanted to be a missionary doctor until I found out I'd need about twelve additional years of training after high school. But I also wanted a house with a wrap-around porch, in the country, with beautiful mountain views. Family friends of ours, the Campbells, had such a home. It was picture perfect. A yellow country home with the most beautiful views, and a wrap-around porch.

Yellow is one of my favorite colors because it's just so happy. I chose yellow and white as our wedding colors, and I painted a wall in our first home bright yellow as well. Joel said he felt like he was living in a clown's house when I added bright blue on the adjoining wall. So eventually I went to a nice neutral color for both of them. Interior decorating is not one of my giftings.

Because our family was friends with the Campbells, we were guests at their house a number of times. We even had Thanksgiving with them once in their perfectly peaceful, beautiful home. I told my older sister, Melissa, that if I could choose any house to live in, it would be the Campbell's.

Fast forward about twenty-seven years. My dad told me the Campbell's house was going to be listed. Joel and I figured it would be out of our price range, but I sent Mr. Campbell a text letting him know we were interested in his home. He invited us over, and after walking through every room, it was as I suspected. I was in love.

How could we afford it though? I had quit my job, was spending lots of money on doctor's visits and supplements. Joel had just started a new job that paid less and didn't provide benefits. I heard God tell me to follow Joel's lead. I thought that would mean to let it go, but to my surprise, Joel kept pursuing it! We looked over our budget, Mr. Campbell came down in price for us, and somehow, we qualified for the loan we would need to make it work. On August 4th, 2020, I called Mr. Campbell with an offer to buy his home. He accepted, and we moved in on October 31st!

We call it our *miracle home* because that's what it is. As I write, we will have lived here for one year and not a single day has gone by that I have not been in awe that I get to call this place home. Joel and I still aren't sure how it all worked out. Going from a two-income household down to one, and with that one making less money than before, makes this a *but God* story in our lives. Joel said that God made it so that He gets the glory because in the natural, it doesn't make sense.

USED TO WORKING

I've worked since I was ten years old. It began when a friend and I both wanted to save money to buy a horse. We put signs up on the mailboxes that read, "We'll work odd jobs: scooping horse poop, babysitting, etc. because we want to buy a horse!" We got a lot of jobs and worked very hard. By the time I was twelve, I'd saved up $2,000 and kept it safe in my sock drawer.

I continued to work through my junior high, high school, and college years. I babysat a whole lot, taught piano lessons, instructed dance classes, and led worship whenever I was asked to. At Cracker Barrel, I worked as a hostess, cashier, and server. I served at a steakhouse in Texas, and became an administrative assistant at church, which eventually led to being on staff there as a pastor.

I didn't stop working when I had children. I worked as a mother to all four of them, until Gracie was eight months old. That's when I became too sick to continue. I say all this because I was used to earning an income. I liked being able to contribute financially. And when I knew I needed to stop working, fear rose up in me. How was I going to pay for my doctor's appointments?

A month before I resigned, I told Joel that one of my hesitations with resigning was knowing our income would decrease. I broke down one day as we were driving, bawling because I'd held so much fear in and finally let out the stress of keeping my worries concealed. Joel kindly told me I was believing a lie. Whether or not I made money, I'd get the help my body needed. And for the last two years, God hasn't let me work. He told me, "I am your provider." Really, He always has been, but now that I can't work, I've faced the poverty mentality I've lived with for too long.

If I say I trust God, shouldn't that include trusting Him to provide for my *every* need? God owns the cattle on a thousand hills (Psalm 50:10), so why do we ever doubt His ability to provide for us? One of the names of God is Jehovah Jireh, which means God will provide.

I want to encourage those who sense the Lord leading you into something new but are struggling to trust how it will work out. God blesses our obedience to Him. He can make a way where there seems to be no way! He is a miracle-working God, remember? If He can rain down food from heaven, He can figure out how to provide for your financial needs. I love the simple lyrics of this Don Moen song, "Trust and obey, for there's no other way, to be happy in Jesus, but to trust and obey."

Back to the house story...

God knew the desire of my heart that had been there since childhood. And when I needed it the most, He made it come true. Had we moved here during an easy time of our lives, I don't think it would have meant the same to us as it does now, because of the season we've been in.

Married friends of ours visited shortly after we moved, and the wife said to me, "This is your house of healing." Yes. Yes, it is. This home is confirmation God knows the desires of my heart and that He goes above and beyond my expectations. It's a reminder that God is loving, faithful, kind, generous, and good, even in the midst of trials and pain. His timing is perfect. He is not slow in keeping His promises, even when it feels that way.

A DETAILED GOD

For as long as I can remember, I wanted a white horse. I planned on naming it Spirit. When we moved into our home, guess what came galloping through our neighbor's yard? A beautiful, white, thoroughbred horse! I asked his owner what his name was, and he said, "Holy, like in church."

I was stunned. What are the chances of a white horse named Holy practically living in our backyard!? Put his name and what I wanted to name a white horse together and you get "Holy Spirit!" Ha! You can't make this stuff up! It felt like an extra kiss from heaven, something so detailed only God could have arranged it.

40

He is into the details of our lives. He knows the seemingly small things that bring us joy. I love this about Him.

We lived in our previous home for 10 years and it never felt the way this home felt after just a couple of days. We'd barely lived here yet it instantly became home! It just felt right and caused me to think about heaven and how perfect it will feel. If an earthly home could evoke a sense of belonging, how much more will my forever home feel that way?

The truth is God is no respecter of persons. He doesn't show favoritism. If He did this for me, He can do it for you too. If He cares about the details in my life, He cares about the details in your life as well. He's known every dream in your heart from the time you were a little kid. He has not forgotten about them.

I think I'm a pretty good mom. I love my kids fiercely! Out of my love for them, I want to make their dreams come true. I listen to their wants and figure out ways to bring them to life. If I, being human and imperfect, desire to bless my children and see their dreams fulfilled, how much more does God want this for us, His children, since He is the perfect parent?

Perhaps you have given up on those childhood dreams, thinking they could never come to pass. Let this be a reminder to you that God has not forgotten them. It might be taking longer than you want, but speaking from experience, His timing really is perfect.

Our Miracle House

Weeping may endure for a night,
But joy comes in the morning.
Psalm 30:5b (NKJV)

Chapter 5

Purpose in the Waiting

"But those who wait on the LORD shall
renew their strength; They shall mount up with
wings like eagles, they shall run and not be
weary, they shall walk and not faint."
Isaiah 40:31 (NKJV)

Waiting is not easy, but it's often required of us. Some of you have been waiting for a long time, and you're beginning to question whether or not things will ever change. Believe me when I say I understand, and I feel for you. Every night when I lie down to sleep, I await the day my face won't be in discomfort. And every morning when I wake up, I hope it's the day I'll feel like myself again.

Waiting is difficult. If only God would act according to my time-line. I've told Him repeatedly, "Okay, it's time for You to heal me. Your turn. Your time to shine. It's past time, God. Today would be a great day for my miracle, etc." Am I the only one who has noticed God never seems to be in a hurry?

That makes me think of the story of Lazarus. John 11:1–7 (NKJV) reads this way. *"Now a certain man was sick, Lazarus of Bethany, the town of Mary and her sister Martha. It was that Mary who anointed the Lord with fragrant oil and wiped His feet with her hair, whose brother Lazarus was sick. Therefore, the sisters sent to Him, saying, 'Lord, behold, he whom You love is sick.' When Jesus heard that, He said, 'This sickness is not unto death, but for the glory of God, that the Son of God may be glorified through it.' Now Jesus loved Martha and her sister and Lazarus. So, when He heard that he was sick, He stayed two more days in the place where He was. Then after this He said to the disciples, 'Let us go to Judea again.'"*

When Jesus heard that Lazarus was sick, He stayed in the place where He was for two more days. He was not in a hurry to respond.

Now let's jump to verses 17–23. *"So when Jesus came, He found that he had already been in the tomb four days. Now Bethany was near Jerusalem, about two miles away. And many of the Jews had joined the women around Martha and Mary, to comfort them concerning their brother. Then Martha, as soon as she heard that Jesus was coming, went and met Him, but Mary was sitting in the house. Now Martha said to Jesus, 'Lord, if You had been here, my brother would not have died. But even now I know that whatever You ask of God, God will give You.' Jesus said to her, 'Your brother will rise again.'"*

We'll skip ahead and finish by reading verses 32–44. *"Then, when Mary came where Jesus was, and saw Him, she fell down at His feet, saying to Him, 'Lord, if You had been here, my brother would not have died.' Therefore, when Jesus saw her weeping, and the Jews who came with her weeping, He groaned in the spirit and was troubled. And He said, 'Where have you laid him?' They said to Him, 'Lord, come and see.' Jesus wept. Then the Jews said, 'See how He loved him!' And some of them said, 'Could not this Man, who opened the eyes of the blind, also have kept this man from* dying?' Then Jesus, again groaning in Himself, came to the tomb. It was a cave, and a stone lay against it. Jesus said, 'Take away the stone.' Martha, the sister of him who was dead, said to Him, 'Lord, by this time there is a stench, for he has been dead four days.' Jesus said to her, 'Did I not say to you that if you would believe you would see the glory of God?' Then they took away the stone from the place where the dead man was lying. And Jesus lifted up His eyes and said, 'Father, I thank You that You have heard Me. And I know that You always hear Me, but because of the people who are standing by I said this, that they may believe that You sent Me.' Now when He had said these things, He cried with a loud voice, 'Lazarus, come forth!' And he who had died came out bound hand and foot with graveclothes, and his face was wrapped with a cloth. Jesus said to them, 'Loose him, and let him go.'"

THIS STORY ROCKS MY WORLD! We could spend so much time going through the many powerful truths from it, but I want to focus on Jesus' timing.

He could have gone to Lazarus the moment he learned of his sickness. Or he could have sent the word for him to be healed, as he did for the Roman Centurion's servant. Lazarus would have been restored to health. But instead, He waited. Why? He tells us why.

Jesus said it was for the glory of God. He knew a miracle was going to take place, and it would build faith in many. So instead of doing what everyone hoped He would do, following their way and their timing, He waited for God's best timing. He didn't just heal Lazarus. He brought him back to life!

Some miracles happen instantly. Others take time. God knows which way is best in your situation. I've been crying out for a miracle every day. A sign in my home declares, "There Will Be Miracles." My children pray for them daily too. Even though I haven't had an instant miracle yet, I see God using this time of waiting for good. I know my miracle is coming. Of course, I wish it had already happened.

But what if, as in the story of Lazarus, Jesus doesn't just want to heal me, but instead transform my life and the lives of those around me!?

I wouldn't be writing right now if I was already healed. I wouldn't be singing the new songs God planted in my heart. I wouldn't have learned the valuable lesson of compassion for those who have suffered, especially with chronic illnesses. When I pastored, I didn't know how to pray for people who struggled with ongoing health issues. I had never experienced that trial so I didn't know what they needed from me. But now I do.

Recently I prayed for a woman at the park who has been battling stage four cancer for many years. As I prayed for her, I didn't struggle to find words, because I now understand suffering. I know what it feels like to be in pain every hour of every day, for years on end. I know the thoughts that run through your mind, the mental battle that's constantly being fought, the fight to hold on to hope, and the fight to choose joy. I get it now and I'm more compassionate because I understand how hard it is to not feel well.

I can't wait for the day I can go to someone in need and clean their toilets or cook them homemade turkey soup for five weeks straight. But until that day comes, I will continue to look for and find the good that is coming out of this season.

PURPOSE REVEALED

My children are full of faith and compassion because of what I've walked through. They pray for people every single night, believing for their miracles. They pray for people by name. "Jesus, heal Michelle. Take away her dizziness." "Jesus, touch Jane. Help her to feel better." "Jesus, take away the cancer in Roxanne's body." "Jesus, help mom to be fully healed." "Jesus, work a miracle in Abi's body." "God, please help Uncle Matt to feel better." They are my heroes in the faith because they are kind when people are suffering and don't give up praying for those in need.

Had it not been for the trial I've had to endure, we would not have declared our house a house of miracles where we prayed for the sick every day. It's been hard waiting, but so much good has occurred through the process. And, I have to believe that God not rushing my miracle is because there's greater purpose in the waiting.

God has a purpose in your waiting too. Don't give up. Your life can change in a day. The moment I'm all back to normal, this season of suffering will become a memory, and I'll be so thankful I didn't quit when the season felt long.

I thought I was going to be married by the time I was nineteen or twenty. I had my life planned out. So, when those years passed by, I became pretty discontent being unmarried. I *desperately* wanted "my man" to come along. I heard God tell me I would be twenty-five when I wed, and I was like, "That must not be you, Lord." Ha! Of course, He was right. I was twenty-five years old, which, honestly, is still very young.

My junior high pastor said my life could change in a day. She was referring to the day I'd meet my husband. She was right. My life changed the moment Joel Scott came up to me at church. He said, "Hi, I'm Joel, and I've been wanting to meet you."

I had waited for what felt like forever to meet *Mr. Right*, and finally it happened. It was not in my timing, but in God's. And I'm so glad I didn't settle for anything less than God's best. I once heard a quote that has stuck with me: "Best's worst enemy is good, in the fact of time." We can rush things in life and settle for the good. Or we can wait on the Lord and receive His best.

Maybe God is getting ready for a *Lazarus come forth! It's time to take the graveclothes off* moment in your circumstance! What was Lazarus' part in coming back to life? It was simply obedience to Jesus' voice. Jesus gave the command to come forth. Lazarus obeyed by standing up, responding to the voice of His friend and Savior, and stepping out of that tomb. What is Jesus asking you to do in this season of waiting? What graveclothes bind you that He is commanding to be loosed? Are you bound in fear, or wrapped up in worry? It's time to be free!

If Jesus can raise a dead man—a fully stinky, dead for four days man—then surely, He can work a miracle in your life too. And if He's having you wait, there's a reason for it. He's working it all out for your good and His glory!

I have to believe that God not rushing my miracle
is because there's greater purpose in the waiting.

But as for me, I trust in You, O LORD;
I say, "You are my God." My times are in Your hand...
Psalm 31:14-15a (NKJV)

Chapter 6

From Thriving to Surviving

*"My flesh and my heart fail; but God is the
strength of my heart and my portion forever."*
Psalm 73:26 (NKJV)

When I was young, I came up with a list of *one-hundred things to do before I die*. The list consisted of things like riding an elephant, going skydiving, eating bread and cheese in Germany, meeting the president, running a marathon, riding a camel in Egypt, and on and on and on.

Dreaming was once very easy for me. I dreamt of getting married, traveling, conquering mountains, writing a book, and recording new songs. And even more, I had the aspiration and drive to see them through. Then I got sick, and the only thing I dreamed about was feeling normal again. Nothing made me excited anymore. I went from being carefree and thriving, to simply surviving. Every single day turned into survival mode. I'd get up with the kids at seven in the morning and think, "I just have to make it to naptime." Naptime ended and I'd think, "I just have to make it until after dinner and then I can lie down again." And after dinner I'd think, "I just have to get the kids in bed, and then I'll be in my bed."

I felt rough and looked rough too. I lost twenty-one pounds and it wasn't flattering. Being compared to a skeleton is not a compliment. The *no-butt-baggy-pants* look isn't cute. I'm going to digress for just a moment.

The last eight months or so I've been able to keep on some weight. Since I was at my lowest, I've gained thirty-seven pounds and I'm thankful for it! I'd rather have a little extra on me than not enough. Don't let a little chub on your tub get you down. I'd have taken a little extra in a heartbeat when I looked like a stick.

I didn't wear makeup often because the nerves in my face were so sensitive that it hurt to apply it, and my balance was so distorted that makeup lines were hard to manage. It hurt to style my hair. So for a long time I never dried or curled it. It's been almost two years since I've been to the salon. My scalp was super sensitive, and although it's been said that beauty is pain, it doesn't mean that it's worth it. All of this is to say that not only did I not feel good, I didn't look good either. When I saw my reflection in a mirror, I'd think to myself, "What has happened to me? How did I go from being a capable, strong, aspiring Proverbs-thirty-one-type woman, to someone who could no longer get ready each day?"

There's one moment that stands out in my mind, and in a way, I still feel the pain of it. My sweet Esther asked me to help put on her coat, and the task of bending down felt overwhelming. I thought, "Oh God, You gave me these precious four children, and I am struggling to button up their coats? This can't be." When my kids asked me to make them a smoothie, or get them a glass of water, I felt fear rise because it meant that I'd have to stand up and walk. I felt too dizzy to read to my little ones.

When Hannah (my younger sister) came over twice a week, she'd sometimes say she didn't feel like she did much to help. I'd explain to her that everything she did was helpful, getting salt for the kid's food, changing Gracie's diapers, making mac n' cheese. Anything I didn't have to do was a relief for me. And man–oh–man was that depressing. I love taking care of my kids. And I love to clean our home. I love having things to do, projects to work on, parties to plan, and having people over. Then suddenly, everything I loved to do felt like a struggle.

One of the most difficult parts about this journey has been not feeling myself. I went from being energized by people to being *afraid* to be around them. I felt like I was forced into being an introvert. If I was around anyone other than my family and close friends, I'd be overwhelmed. My body would start to panic which created bizarre neurological symptoms and I'd need to lie down. It was as if my brain couldn't handle the stimulation and many times, I felt like I was on the brink of a nervous breakdown. I remember a church service when it was so hard to stand that I had to sit during worship and the crowd caused everything around me to feel like a blur. I wept. I couldn't believe I didn't even want to be at church anymore.

At one point I thought, "Sucks to be me. Man, it sucks to be me." Pardon my language, but I think it's important to be honest. It would be really easy to look at my Instagram feed or Facebook profile and assume the struggle hasn't been that bad. But if I'm telling the truth, this season has challenged me in every possible way.

ADDRESSING THE LIES

I have never doubted the existence of God, but throughout this time of health challenges I have questioned His love for me. I've wondered if He's forgotten about me. I assumed that because I wasn't healed yet, He figured I wasn't worth healing. I wondered if my sin had caused me to be sick. I even entertained the lie that I would bring more glory to God dead than alive. Is this too honest for you? I hope not because my heart in sharing is if you've battled these same lies, we can address them together. And we can learn to never fall for them again.

John 9:1–5 (NKJV) says, *"Now as Jesus passed by, He saw a man who was blind from birth. And His disciples asked Him, saying, 'Rabbi, who sinned, this man or his parents, that he was born blind?' Jesus answered, 'Neither this man nor his parents sinned, but that the works of God should be revealed in him. I must work the works of Him who sent Me while it is day; the night is coming when no one can work. As long as I am in the world, I am the light of the world.'"*

Was this man born blind because of sin? The answer is no, but rather so the works of God would be revealed in him. Jesus made mud with His spit and dirt, put it on the blind man's eyes, and had him go wash it off. The man came back seeing. The miraculous power of God was revealed through him. I have asked God multiple times if I'm sick because of my sin. Every time I've asked, He has responded with, "No." *Thank you, God, for Your mercy.*

We need to be careful never to apply the Bible to prove or confirm a self-motivated narrative. We mustn't take Scripture out of context, twisting it to align with our values, to prove a point or make us feel better about ourselves or our actions. Rather, we must look at the Word as a whole.

God desires us to live righteously and He's looking for those who diligently seek Him. I don't want to ignore the fact there are consequences for the choices and sins we make. But friend, Jesus was sent to heal the sick, not make people ill for messing up.

Matthew 4:23 (ESV) says, *"And he went throughout all Galilee, teaching in their synagogues and proclaiming the gospel of the kingdom and healing every disease and every affliction among the people."* Luke 4:40 (NKJV) says, *"When the sun was setting, all those who had any that were sick with various diseases brought them to Him; and He laid His hands on every one of them and healed them."* Jesus took our pain and bore our suffering when He went to the cross. He was beaten so we could be whole and whipped so we could be healed (Isaiah 53:4). Jesus carried the weight of the world's sin. He became sin who knew no sin (2 Corinthians 5:21) so we could be made right with God. He became the sacrifice.

Through my study of the Word, I believe sin has consequences that sometimes result in physical hardship, but Jesus doesn't make you sick. Because He came to set us free, I can never agree with someone who says He binds people with illness to teach them a lesson. *That's not the heart of our Savior.*

The devil is a liar. In fact, he is the father of lies (John 8:44). He wants to trap you in the lies he sets for you and take you out, because he knows God's plan for you is *good.* He would love to convince you that God is punishing you with suffering and doesn't want you well. Those are lies that need to be addressed.

I'm sorry to tell you this, but you are hated. The devil hates you and he hates your faith in God. He is all about getting you to doubt the Lord and His great love for you. His plan is to make you believe your life will never get better, the best is behind you, and you are not worth fighting for. I know this, because he has tried over and over again to convince me I should just give up. He knows I will never walk away from my faith in God. So instead he has tried to take me out before my time, by speaking lies. "Your husband deserves a healthy wife. Your kids would be better off with a mom who can run with them. You'll never feel normal again. Your life will always be a struggle." *These are lies!!* And I'm bettin' he's been lying to you too. Confront the lies and declare God's truth over them. It's time to take a stand against the tactics of the enemy. It's time to suit up in the armor of God.

SUIT UP

Ephesians 6:10–18 gives us a strategy to come against the enemy. I like how the NLT reads, *"A final word: Be strong in the Lord and in his mighty power. Put on all of God's armor so that you will be able to stand firm against all strategies of the devil. For we are not fighting against flesh-and-blood enemies, but against evil rulers and authorities of the unseen world, against mighty powers in this dark world, and against evil spirits in the heavenly places. Therefore, put on every piece of God's armor so you will be able to resist the enemy in the time of evil. Then after the battle you will still be standing firm. Stand your ground, putting on the belt of truth and the body armor of God's righteousness. For shoes, put on the peace that comes from the Good News so that you will be fully prepared. In addition to all of these, hold up the shield of faith to stop the fiery arrows of the devil. Put on salvation as your helmet, and take the sword of the Spirit, which is the word of God. Pray in the Spirit at all times and on every occasion. Stay alert and be persistent in your prayers for all believers everywhere."*

Let's go over the armor in the order we are encouraged to put it on:

The *belt of truth* is first. We must know the truth to be victorious over the enemy. It's the truth that sets us free (John 8:32). We are to fasten it around us, securing it in place. The belt of a soldier held his sword. The truth and the Word go hand in hand. God's Word is truth. Jesus is the way, the truth, and the life (John 14:6). And it must be a part of the daily armor we put on to be ready for battle.

Then *righteousness*. It acts as a shield over our heart. Right living protects us, keeping us from harm. Our obedience to the Lord and living in a way that honors Him opens the door to blessing in our lives.

We are to walk in *peace*. Peace is a weapon against the enemy. When we choose peace over fear, we are trampling on the enemy's plan to disrupt our lives.

Then we are to hold up the *shield of faith*, having it ready! In the New King James Version, Ephesians 6:16 says, *"Above all, taking the shield of faith with which you will be able to quench all the fiery darts of the wicked one."* Above all, take up the shield of faith. This is a strong statement and one we should pay attention to. Faith is a weapon against the fiery darts of the enemy. When his lies come in contact with our shield of faith, they fall to the ground, unable to penetrate us. Above all, have this piece of armor ready!

We are to put on the *helmet of salvation*. The helmet covers our mind—our thoughts. This is so important in our battle plan. If our thoughts are out of alignment with truth, we are subject to all sorts of attacks. We must saturate our mind in the Word of God, and daily put on our helmet of salvation. It's what reminds us of who and whose we are.

The *sword of the Spirit* is our weapon of offense. We come against the enemy with the Word of God. His truth. That's why it's so important to know the Word. When the enemy attacks, we counterattack with the Word of God.

Jesus showed us how to do this in Matthew 4:1–11 (NKJV). *"Then Jesus was led up by the Spirit into the wilderness to be tempted by the devil. And when He had fasted forty days and forty nights, afterward He was hungry. Now when the tempter came to Him, he said, 'If You are the Son of God, command that these stones become bread.' But He answered and said, 'It is written, "Man shall not live by bread alone, but by every word that proceeds from the mouth of God."' Then the devil took Him up into the holy city, set Him on the pinnacle of the temple, and said to Him, 'If You are the Son of God, throw Yourself down. For it is written: "He shall give His angels charge over you," and, "In their hands they shall bear you up, lest you dash your foot against a stone."'*

"Jesus said to him, 'It is written again, "You shall not tempt the Lord your God."' Again, the devil took Him up on an exceedingly high mountain, and showed Him all the kingdoms of the world and their glory. And he said to Him, 'All these things I will give You if You will fall down and worship me.' Then Jesus said to him, 'Away with you, Satan! For it is written, "You shall worship the Lord your God, and Him only you shall serve."' Then the devil left Him, and behold, angels came and ministered to Him."

The devil tried three times to persuade Jesus to listen to him. Jesus knew the Word and answered Satan with it. What happened? The devil left Him, and angels came and ministered to Jesus. Boom! That's how it's done. When the devil comes to you with his scheming and lies, you answer back, "God's Word says..."

MORE TACTICS OF THE ENEMY

Another tactic of the enemy is to cause feelings of guilt and shame. This tactic has also been used against me. I've felt a crushing amount of guilt this season. I haven't been able to be the friend I want to be. I wish I could work out with Joel and we could go on amazing adventures together. I've thought about my mother-in-love and how much she's taken care of my kids and me, and I've felt guilty about it. Even though she's always willing and wants to help, I've thought, "She deserves a normal daughter-in-love." I take a nap every day. For a long time, I felt guilty about it. I'd tell my older kids, "Okay, it's time for Gracie and Mommy's nap." And then I'd lie in bed wishing I felt good enough to stay up with them. Mom guilt has been in full swing.

I see how the enemy has worked to defeat me, and I am determined to not let him win. He's shown his hand, his every lie. I call his bluff. I choose life.

Deuteronomy 30:19-20 (MSG) says, *"I call Heaven and Earth to witness against you today: I place before you Life and Death, Blessing and Curse. Choose life so that you and your children will live. And love GOD, your God, listening obediently to him, firmly embracing him. Oh yes, he is life itself, a long life settled on the soil that GOD, your God, promised to give your ancestors, Abraham, Isaac, and Jacob."*

I choose life and blessing for my family and me. I know I'm not the only one the enemy has lied to and tried to burden with guilt and shame. As I said before, my assumption is he lies to you too, and that is why we must know the truth.

What is the truth for me? The truth is that God wants me well. Jesus was sent to earth, fully God yet fully man, and He spent his years of ministry teaching truth, healing bodies, and setting captives free. Jesus only did what He saw His Father doing. If Jesus was commissioned by His Father to heal, then I know it is not His heart for me to be sick. The truth is that even though I don't feel normal yet, life is worth living. God's plan for me is good. I am more than a conqueror (Romans 8:37).

What is the truth for you? What has God spoken to you? What have you read in His Word that you need to cling to right now and not let the enemy steal from you?

When the devil comes to you with his scheming and lies, you answer back, "God's Word says..." It's strange to go from being someone who loves to dream, to someone who just hopes they make it through the day without falling apart. The tears from my entire life would not equal what the last two and a half years have produced. But I remain confident of this. I will see the goodness of the Lord, in the land of the living (Psalm 27:13).

I will see God's goodness. I am seeing it now. Even though this has felt like a season of surviving, I am seeing in the midst of it, dreams coming true. We live in a fallen world—a world full of sin—so it's not going to be perfect. We are promised trials, and we often forget that. But Jesus! He overcomes this world (John 16:33). Because of Jesus and the goodness of God, we can be in a trial and at the same time experience His faithfulness. That's what's happening in my life right now.

DREAMS HAVE COME TRUE IN A SEASON MARKED BY TEARS.

I've already talked about our house, and that it's a dream come true. But the fact that I planted more flowers this year, that we got a dozen chickens, and that we are eating their eggs is, too. I highly encourage anyone on the fence about getting chickens to just go for it! It's almost magical to collect eggs from them. And it's so much fun giving those fresh eggs away.

A friend gave me a sourdough starter so I'm making bread—something I've wanted to do for a long time. We have land. So much of it that we needed to get a riding lawnmower. The first time Joel mowed the lawn with it, he said, "This is a dream come true." I'm a full-time mom, able to homeschool my kids. We aren't rushing out the door every day. My house isn't always a disaster! We're going to plant fruit trees next spring. We're planning for a garden. I'm going to plant lots of wildflowers and give them away to people when they visit. We're going to have a patch of pumpkins. These are all dreams coming to pass. And they will come to pass in a season that's been marked by tears.

God works in mysterious ways! And though life is hard right now, I recognize His goodness and His faithfulness to me. When we pray together as a family every night, I say, "God, we trust You." And I thank Him for His faithfulness to us. I don't understand why I'm still in pain, but I'm learning that you really can have joy in the midst of sorrow.

YOU CAN GRIEVE AND BE THANKFUL AT THE SAME TIME.

On our family vacation last summer, I felt like I was processing all sorts of emotions and it wasn't because of *that-time-of-the-month*, if you know what I mean. It was this wrestling of thankfulness and grief. I felt so thankful to be making memories with my family, but I felt such sorrow over not feeling myself while making them.

The previous year I wasn't able to go away with Joel and the kids much and the times I did were very difficult for me. Once we went to a cabin for about a week, and I had to grip the table legs with my own to sit upright. I'd lie in bed for three hours during the day and lie down again right after dinner. It didn't exactly feel like vacationing. When we went away this past summer, I was able to do more with my family and good memories were made. But I was still in pain and didn't feel normal so I found myself in a constant wrestling match between thanksgiving and grief. Until I realized that it didn't have to be a fight. I could feel both at the same time and that that was okay.

Jesus modeled this when He was in the Garden of Gethsemane (Matthew 26:39). He prayed to God that what He was being asked to do (His impending death on the cross) would pass from Him, yet not His will but God's be done. But we also read in Hebrews 12:2 that it was for the joy set before Him that He endured the cross. Jesus didn't want to go through the pain, yet He endured it because of the joy that was coming. He experienced both sorrow and trust, pain and purpose.

It comforts me to know that even Jesus asked if there could be a different way, if the cup could pass from Him. So in my moments of crying out to God to make the pain go away, I rest in knowing Jesus can relate with me. He relates with your pain too. He understands sorrow. Isaiah 53:3 (NKJV) says, *"He is despised and rejected by men, a Man of sorrows and acquainted with grief."*

Jesus endured it all, and I'm sure if you asked Him, He'd say it was worth it. Resurrection life followed His trust and surrender. Life will follow your trust and surrender too.

THE BIG WHY

Why do bad things happen to good people? I've asked this question, too. Why do amazing people get cancer and die, when abusers seemingly get away with it and enjoy the rest of their lives? Have you ever felt this way? Like the wicked prosper while you suffer? The answer goes back to the fact we live in a fallen world. Bad things happen because this world is not our permanent home. It's not heaven. If we live constantly doubting the faithfulness of God based on difficult circumstances, we'll miss out on a beautiful walk of faith with Him. He is after my heart and yours. He wants us to know Him and live in an awareness of His presence.

Just because He doesn't answer your prayers the way you want Him to, doesn't mean He isn't listening. It doesn't mean He isn't fully aware. He knows best and sometimes it won't make sense to us.

I want to encourage those of you who feel like you're simply surviving right now. That dreaming feels impossible, and the future looks hopeless because you only have the energy to make it through the day. My dear friend, Steffani, once said that every breath is breakthrough. She's right. Some days, all you can do is breathe. But friend, *that* is something. Keep breathing. Take it one breath at a time, one hour at a time, one day at a time. Eventually, you will dream again. Writing this book feels like dreaming to me. I'm beginning to have hope for the future. I'm starting to see the good that will come.

Eggs from our chickens!

If I can dream while weeping, so can you. And one day, our weeping will turn to joy. Our sorrow will transform into dancing (Psalm 30:11). I believe this for you and for me. It's okay if you don't have the faith for it right now. I'll be the friend who removes the tiles on the roof for you. I'll stand in faith and carry you to Jesus, knowing He will not disappoint.

It's okay to cry and at the same time give thanks. Actually, I think it leads to healing. Give yourself permission to weep, and know that while you do, not one tear is lost on the Lord. He will restore what's been stolen (Joel 2:25). Yes, I believe this for you and for me.

Esther in her happy place

Chapter 7

Just One Touch

"For she said, 'If only I may touch His clothes,
I shall be made well.'"
Mark 5:28 (NKJV)

One of the stories from the Bible that has ministered to me the most in this season is the story of the woman with the issue of blood. Mark 5 is where you'll find it.

A certain woman had bled for twelve years and had gone to many physicians. She'd spent all the money she had trying to get better, but instead of getting better, she just got worse. She heard about Jesus and knew He was in town, so she went to see Him. A massive crowd surrounded Him. What she did in the midst of her pain and the crowds that surrounded Jesus is truly inspiring.

In Mark 5:28–34 (NKJV), she was determined to press through the crowd. *"For she said, 'If only I may touch His clothes, I shall be made well.' Immediately the fountain of her blood was dried up, and she felt in her body that she was healed of the affliction. And Jesus, immediately knowing in Himself that power had gone out of Him, turned around in the crowd and said, 'Who touched*

My clothes?' But His disciples said to Him, 'You see the multitude thronging You, and You say, "Who touched Me?"' And He looked around to see her who had done this thing. But the woman, fearing and trembling, knowing what had happened to her, came and fell down before Him and told Him the whole truth. And He said to her, 'Daughter, your faith has made you well. Go in peace, and be healed of your affliction.'"

This woman desperately wanted to be healed. She knew enough about Jesus to know that if she could just touch Him, just one touch, she could receive her miracle. Her passion caused her to push through the crowd. Her desperation to be healed and touch Jesus gave her the determination and strength she needed to reach for Him. Her burning desire to be healed drew her to Jesus. And in turn, He not only healed her. He spoke courage over her.

When you read this story in the King James Version, Jesus tells her to be of good comfort (Luke 8:48). If you look up the root of those words, you'll find Jesus is telling her to have courage and to be of good cheer. Oh, how kind our Savior is!

In Mark 5:30, Jesus asked who touched him. The word *touch* in this verse is the Greek word *haptomai* which means to fasten to and make adhere to. The root comes from the word *hapto* and it specifically means to fasten fire to a thing, to kindle, to set on fire. This woman's desperation to touch Jesus burned through her and that fire-like touch caused Jesus to stop in His tracks. Her desperation for Him did not end in disappointment. She was healed and received encouragement from Jesus as He spoke to her. He went above and beyond her expectations by not only healing her, but by talking to her face-to-face.

Jesus said He felt power going out from Him! The word *power* is the Greek word *dunamis* which is where we get the word dynamite. How does dynamite ignite? You set the wick on fire! What an amazing thought! The woman touched Jesus with a fire-like touch that caused *dunamis* power to leave His body and make her whole. The fire in her set off the dynamite in Him!

The fire in her set off the dynamite in Him!

Do we have that same kind of fire-like passion for Jesus, for His touch on our lives? The kind that would cause Him to stop what He's doing and speak to us? I've asked this about myself. Do I have that kind of desperation—the kind that would drive me to press through every obstacle to get close to Jesus and receive His healing touch?

After she was healed, the woman realized she couldn't hide. She came to Jesus, trembling. She told Him, as well as the crowd that surrounded them, what had happened. She wasn't expecting to be singled out, BUT JESUS wanted to speak to her. He could have felt the power leave His body and moved on, but he waited for her to come to Him. Then in front of everyone He called her *daughter*, told her to have courage, and affirmed it was faith that had made her whole. How powerful! Daughter here means *acceptable to God, rejoicing in God's peculiar care and protection*. Whoa! Think about that for a moment and let it sink in. He called her acceptable and rejoiced in her care and protection.

The footnote from Luke 8:43–48 says, "Many people surrounded Jesus as he made his way toward Jairus' house. It was virtually impossible to get through the multitude, but one woman fought her way desperately through the crowd in order to touch Jesus. As soon as she did so, she was healed. What a difference there is between crowds that are curious about Jesus and the few who reach out and touch Him! It isn't that Jesus didn't know who had touched him; it's that he wanted the woman to step forward and identify herself. Jewish men carefully avoided touching, speaking to or even looking at women in this condition. By contrast, Jesus proclaimed to hundreds of people that this unclean woman had touched him, and then he healed her. This suffering woman was not overlooked."

For some of you, Jesus wants you to stop hiding, He wants to call you daughter, heal you, remove all shame, speak to you, and bring freedom to your life. You will not be overlooked. You are worthy of His love! You are worth His time and attention.

Have you ever thought, "There's so much going on in the world, my problems don't matter to God? I'm not worth His time?" That's not true! God cares about the details of your life. Jesus was on His way to heal a little girl when He took the time to speak with this woman who had just been healed. This is aside from the fact, but the girl Jesus was on His way to heal was twelve years old. The woman who touched the hem of Jesus' garment had been suffering for twelve years. Coincidence? I don't think so.

By the time Jesus got to the little girl, she was presumed dead, BUT JESUS. He spoke to her saying, *Talitha Cumi,* which translated is, *Little girl, I say to you arise.* And immediately she stood up and walked! Nothing is impossible for Jesus! He can heal a woman who had been sick for twelve years and raise a twelve-year-old back to life!

God wants us to be on fire for Him, to burn with passion once again. His plan isn't for us to live mediocre, but to live sold-out for His glory. I've noticed in my own life, when going through a crisis, I tend to pray more. I feel an increased desperation for His touch. That's ok. But God desires that out of our love for Him, we would draw close every day, not just when we're in need of something. God will use those crisis times to help bring people back. His desire, however, is that we would know, love, and want Him every single day. He desires intimacy with us.

Many times in healing ministry, people who are being healed will feel heat in the area where restoration is needed. Oftentimes the person praying for God's touch, will feel heat as well. After going through the story of the bleeding woman, and knowing what the word *touch* means, I believe Jesus has a burning desire to touch and heal us. And those who are desperate to be healed have a burning desire to touch Him in return. The sense of heat is a sign and a wonder from above that God is present to heal!

Don't let the crowds deter you from pressing through. Don't let the circumstances around you hold you back from believing Jesus is the answer. Instead, let your desperation for Him give you strength to carry on and reach Him. I pray right now your passion for Jesus will increase and you will be set on fire for Him! I pray for you to receive a miracle, whether it's for your marriage, your health, or an addiction. Wherever you need a breakthrough, I pray in Jesus' name it will be done. One touch from Jesus will change your life forever. Let's pray to receive that touch right now:

Dear Jesus,

We know You are everything we need. You are our Source of healing, peace, joy, restoration, hope, provision, and breakthrough. We ask for Your touch on our lives right now. We pray for dunamis power to be released in us, bringing miraculous breakthrough to our circumstances. We pray our love for You will increase. We pray the desire to be close to You would burn in us, not just when we're going through a trial, but all of the time. We need You! The world needs You. Your touch changes everything. We pray for revival in our lives, our family's lives, in our workplace, and in this world. We need to encounter You. We are desperate for Your touch, Jesus. We pray that starting now, we will be able to testify to Your power at work in our lives.

In Your name we pray and believe. Amen.

You are my hiding place;
You shall preserve me from trouble;
You shall surround me with songs of deliverance.
Psalm 32:7 (NKJV)

Chapter 8

Fire Season

"But He knows the way that I take
[and He pays attention to it]. When He has tried me, I will
come forth as [refined] gold [pure and luminous]."
Job 23:10 (AMP)

Fire is often associated with negative feelings. When it burns through thousands of acres, charring everything in its path, the typical response is not a positive one. That is unless you're like my husband and you've been a wildland firefighter.

Joel worked as a hot shot—quite the fitting title for him, if you ask me. He's told me repeatedly that fire is a necessary part of our ecosystem. Obviously when a fire destroys homes and towns versus open land, it's a different story. But when I've talked about the devastating effects of a fire, he's never expressed the same sense of dread. Instead, he's talked about how fire makes way for new life.

Over the summer we went to the mountains and hiked a trail that had endured a fire some time ago. All of the trees were dead and charred. At first it felt eerie to me, until I began to look at the ground and noticed the growth of new life. Beautiful purple flowers and foliage had begun to cover the ground. The entire time I felt the Lord speaking to me through what I was seeing in the natural, encouraging me to trust Him through this difficult season for new growth was coming for me soon too.

We experience trials and seasons that cause us to feel lifeless, left burnt and charred. Everything around us can look so bleak. We long for the beauty in our lives that we once had. I say *we* because I'm sure I'm not alone in understanding difficult times. As we've discussed, the enemy is quick to lie. He whispers that our lives will never get better, the best is behind us, the fire has taken over, and all we carry is ashes. But, as I hiked that path, with dead trees to my right and left, and burnt dust beneath my feet, I knew God wanted to give me a powerful analogy to continue carrying me through the fiery season. The flowers and foliage reminded me that beauty comes from ashes.

FIRE BRINGS AN AWAKENING

I read an article on the *Britannica* website by Melissa Petruzzello and was blown away by the following: "Some plants, such as the lodgepole pine, Eucalyptus, and Banksia, have serotinous cones or fruits that are completely sealed with resin. These cones and fruits can only open to release their seeds after the heat of a fire has physically melted the resin. Other species, including a number of shrubs and annual plants, require the chemical signals from smoke and charred plant matter to break seed dormancy. Some of these plants will only sprout in the presence of such chemicals and can remain buried in the soil seed bank for decades until a wildfire awakens them."

Isn't that incredible? Certain plants can only bloom when enough heat is present to open them. Seeds that lay dormant are awakened by fire because fire awakens new life. And that growth, as it continues to mature, will overtake everything that's dead.

Beauty blooms out of the ashes. Heat releases new life. You might not see it right away, but there are seeds of hope, healing, peace, joy, and life inside of you that are waiting to blossom.

The ashes you see don't have the final say,
but rather the beauty that lies beneath them.

The burnt ground I saw with new life growing from it.

THE REFINING PROCESS

Just a few months after my health took a wild turn, I heard God tell me that the *refinement* was bringing *alignment*. I was at the start of a time that would test me in ways I never expected. My faith for the miraculous, trust in God's love for me, ability to choose joy, and so much more have been tested. But in doing so, it's led to a strengthening. The areas that have been tried are being refined. And for this, I am thankful.

Did you know fire can't destroy pure gold? It's indestructible. Fire can't destroy what's genuine. One of the desires of my heart is that I would be like gold, purified by the Refiner's fire. Job 23:10 (AMP) says, *"But He knows the way that I take [and He pays attention to it]. When He has tried me, I will come forth as [refined] gold [pure and luminous]."*

Do you remember that old song "Refiner's Fire" by Brian Doerksen?

Purify my heart, let me be as gold and precious silver
Purify my heart, let me be as gold, pure gold
Refiner's fire, my heart's one desire
Is to be holy, set apart for You, Lord
I choose to be holy, set apart for You, my Master
Ready to do Your will
Purify my heart, cleanse me from within
And make me holy
Purify my heart, cleanse me from my sin
Deep within
Refiner's fire, my heart's one desire
Is to be holy, set apart for You, Lord
I choose to be holy, set apart for You, my Master
Ready to do Your will

Times of testing are never fun. But if we allow them to refine us, we will come out shining brightly like pure gold. We will be indestructible. So instead of viewing *fire season* as a negative, remember fire burns chaff away and makes room for new life to grow. Fire brings purification and strengthens us as we yield to the process. Don't forget you can experience fire and come out of it not even smelling like smoke (Daniel 3:27).

The Refinement is Bringing Alignment!

God is our refuge and strength,
A very present help in trouble.
Therefore, we will not fear...
Psalm 46:1-2a (NKJV)

Chapter 9

Praise Precedes Miracles

"About midnight Paul and Silas were praying and singing hymns to God, and the other prisoners were listening to them. Suddenly there was such a violent earthquake that the foundations of the prison were shaken. At once all the prison doors flew open, and everyone's chains came loose."

Acts 16:25-26 (NIV)

It's easy to say God will use every trial we go through for good. It's harder to actually live through that trial. Many things are easier said than done, but it doesn't make them less true. Prior to facing health challenges, I preached about joy. I taught about thankfulness. I shared about having a higher perspective. Joy just came naturally for me because it was a well-developed *muscle* I used daily. But in this season, it's been a challenge. I've spent many days feeling hopeless, crying out to God from morning to night. I've felt like a hypocrite. How could I so easily preach about choosing joy, but now during a trial, I must fight to hold on to it?

Throughout the last couple of years, I've been learning to live out what I truly believe, even when I struggle to feel it. I have learned that joy cannot be based on circumstances, because sometimes life is sweet, but not always. Other times, life can be bitter. Joy cannot be based on how I feel physically. It has to be rooted in something much deeper: the hope of eternal glory, knowing life is but a vapor, and believing God will use everything for good. Even if it doesn't feel good at the time. It's not just an encouraging word we can tell ourselves and others. It's the truth.

PRAISE IN ADVANCE

I have taught about how praise often precedes miracles, and how battles have been won through the power of praise. Let's look at a few examples from the Bible that backs this up.

In 2 Chronicles 20, we read the story of the battle against Jehoshaphat. God orchestrated the victory as Jehoshaphat sent worshippers before his army. Verses 22–24 (NKJV) say, *"Now when they began to sing and to praise, the Lord set ambushes against the people of Ammon, Moab, and Mount Seir, who had come against Judah; and they were defeated. For the people of Ammon and Moab stood up against the inhabitants of Mount Seir to utterly kill and destroy them. And when they had made an end of the inhabitants of Seir, they helped to destroy one another. So when Judah came to a place overlooking the wilderness, they looked toward the multitude; and there were their dead bodies, fallen on the earth. No one had escaped."*

Walls have fallen after a shout of victory. Joshua 6:1–5 (NKJV) confirms it. *"Now Jericho was securely shut up because of the children of Israel; none went out, and none came in. And the Lord said to Joshua: 'See! I have given Jericho into your hand, its king, and the mighty men of valor. You shall march around the city, all you men of war; you shall go all around the city once. This you shall do six days. And seven priests shall bear seven trumpets of rams' horns before the ark. But the seventh day you shall march around the city seven times, and the priests shall blow the trumpets. It shall come to pass, when they make a long blast with the ram's horn, and when you hear the sound of the trumpet, that all the people shall shout with a great shout; then the wall of the city will fall down flat. And the people shall go up every man straight before him.'"*

These are truths I have always believed. Praise is a weapon. It's a battle cry, and it will usher in breakthrough. Having been challenged to live out what I believe and practice what I preached, I'll honestly say I've both succeeded and failed. Some days I've given in to the symptoms and have kept my mouth from shouting forth praise. But the days I have determined to worship God in advance for my breakthrough are the ones where I felt a shift in my spirit and a strengthening of my soul. There is power in praise. It changes the atmosphere.

When we open our mouths in worship—despite how we are feeling—we're inviting heaven to invade earth. The kingdom of heaven is righteousness, peace, and joy. Sorrow lifts as joy takes over. Peace that passes understanding descends on us, and we find it easier to rest. The truth is praise precedes miracles!

I love the story of when Paul and Silas were thrown into prison after casting a demonic spirit out of a fortune teller. This slave girl made a lot of money for her masters. When they realized she had been delivered and was no longer a source of income, they were furious with Paul and Silas. They went straight to the magistrates, saying these two had thrown the city into an uproar.

We'll look at the story in Acts 16:22–26 (NIV). *"The crowd joined in the attack against Paul and Silas, and the magistrates ordered them to be stripped and beaten with rods. After they had been severely flogged, they were thrown into prison, and the jailer was commanded to guard them carefully. When he received these orders, he put them in the inner cell and fastened their feet in the stocks. About midnight Paul and Silas were praying and singing hymns to God, and the other prisoners were listening to them. Suddenly there was such a violent earthquake that the foundations of the prison were shaken. At once all the prison doors flew open, and everyone's chains came loose."*

Once again, praise preceded a miracle. This story is so powerful! Just imagine this setting and the events that led to Paul and Silas being thrown into prison. Through the power of Jesus, these two set a girl with a demonic spirit free. The girl's owners and many others were outraged because they had preached the good news, they endured a severe beating. Then Paul and Silas were thrown into the inner cell of a prison without the freedom to move around, their feet bound in stocks. *And yet*, all of this did not stop them from praising God.

One of the most powerful parts of this story is that the other prisoners were listening to them. The captives were listening to Paul and Silas *pray* and *worship* even in the middle of hardship.

BREAKTHROUGH IN OUR PRAISE

When you and I walk through a trial, never forget those close to us are *watching* and *listening* to our response to suffering. The way we choose to praise God through it will impact others.

In this story about Paul and Silas, not only were they loosed from their bonds, and not only were their prison doors opened, but the Bible says all the prison doors flew open. Everyone's chains came loose. WOW! Praise didn't just precede a miracle for Paul and Silas, it opened the door (literally) for others to experience freedom too. Now that will preach. Your praise is not only powerful in your own life, but it's powerful in the lives of those around you—those watching and listening to your story.

Praise sets captives free. What would have happened had Paul and Silas let their circumstance change their view about God and His calling on their lives? They could have assumed God allowing them to suffer, be severely beaten, be wrongfully accused, and be unjustly thrown into an inner cell, was because He no longer cared about them. Or, they could have let it create doubt in God's goodness and plan for their lives. But instead, they drew close to the Lord in prayer and worship. And it led to a miracle in their lives and freedom to those listening.

The rest of this story in Acts 16:27–35 (NIV) is amazing too. *"The jailer woke up, and when he saw the prison doors open, he drew his sword and was about to kill himself because he thought the prisoners had escaped. But Paul shouted, 'Don't harm yourself! We are all here!' The jailer called for lights, rushed in and fell trembling before Paul and Silas. He then brought them out and asked, 'Sirs, what must I do to be saved?' They replied, 'Believe in the Lord Jesus, and you will be saved—you and your household.' Then they spoke the word of the Lord to him and to all the others in his house. At that hour of the night the jailer took them and washed their wounds; then immediately he and all his household were baptized. The jailer brought them into his house and set a meal before them; he was filled with joy because he had come to believe in God—he and his whole household. When it was daylight, the magistrates sent their officers to the jailer with the order: 'Release those men.'"*

An entire household came to know the Lord because His power caused prison doors to open and bonds to be loosed. A miracle took place after two men chose to focus on the Him instead of their chains. They worshiped instead of worrying and prayed instead of despairing.

Consider too that Paul and Silas could have run out of those doors the second they opened. But their mission was to preach the good news. They had an opportunity to minister to a man desperate to know the Truth. So instead of running from hardship, they waited a little longer.

Let that sink in. They chose to wait a little longer for the sake of another. The guard would have most certainly taken his life.

But instead, he and his household received life. All because Paul and Silas took the time to share the Truth that sets all of us free.

Maybe my time of suffering is to help others who desperately need to know they aren't alone in theirs. Perhaps the trial you have to endure is because it will one day open the prison doors of those who are bound right now. I am choosing to worship through the warfare, and this story shows me it's not only going to lead to my freedom, but freedom for others as well.

Give yourself grace if you've struggled to offer a sacrifice of praise. You can start now. You can start with a simple word of thanksgiving today.

EVERY BREATH IS BREAKTHROUGH

Many times we expect breakthrough moments to be big. But breakthrough for me, over the last couple of years, has looked different. It has been my ability to get out of bed. Put on some lipstick. Read to my children. Make my family dinner. Clean my toilets. Stay up to watch a movie with Joel. And go to bed declaring my body is whole.

Breakthrough has taken place in the times I've turned my eyes heavenward and thanked God for all His goodness to me. It's been in praising Him I get to watch my kids grow and in having a loving husband and an amazing family. It's been in sitting before Him at my piano and letting the tears flow as I've sung, "This is my sacrifice of worship, you deserve it all. It doesn't matter what I feel like, you're worthy of my all." To me, every bit of this is breakthrough. Remember, every breath is breakthrough.

"Every Breath is Breakthrough!" -Steffani Besch

How do you start? Just begin to praise God. Thank Him for everything in your life that is good. Praise Him in advance for how He is going to turn your sorrow into joy, your mourning into dancing.

Blast worship through your home and in your car! If I can praise God in advance for my breakthrough, so can you.

I wrote a song based on Psalm 121:1–2 (NKJV). *"I will lift up my eyes to the hills—From whence comes my help? My help comes from the LORD, who made heaven and earth."* It's an encouragement in the times we feel overwhelmed because we know our help is coming.

The song is a reminder to praise God in advance for breakthrough, to know our stories are not over. Even as we walk through the fire, we can have joy, because it's not just a feeling. It is part of the kingdom of God. As we pray, "Your kingdom come, Your will be done, on earth as it is in heaven," we are inviting joy to invade sorrow. The hope of Heaven then takes over.

Maybe one day we can sing it together. But for now, I pray just reading the lyrics encourages you. I feel led to have you read them out loud. So if you're up for it, please do.

Praise in Advance
Breathe on me, breathe on me
Come revive my weary heart with Your breath
Breathe on me, breathe on me
Come restore my hopeless soul, let it find rest
In You Alone
There's hope on the horizon
There's a reason to lift up my eyes
My help is coming, my help is coming
There's hope on the horizon
There's a reason to let faith arise
My help is coming, I won't give up the fight
Oh it feels so wrong, like times been wasted
And oh I feel overwhelmed and have wondered if I'm gonna make it

But my story's not over, this isn't the end
What I've thought was hopeless
Is where You begin
One day I will tell of, how I've been set free
Of all that has tried to, bury me
Until that day gets here, this is what I'll do
I'm gonna praise You in advance for my breakthrough
I will praise you in advance for my breakthrough

As for me, I will call upon God,
And the LORD shall save me.
Evening and morning and at noon I will pray, and cry aloud,
And He shall hear my voice.
He has redeemed my soul in peace from the battle that was against me.
Psalm 55:16-18a (NKJV)

82

Chapter 10

The Greatest Commandments

*"'And you shall love the Lord your God with all your heart,
with all your soul, with all your mind, and with all your
strength.' This is the first commandment. And the second,
like it, is this: 'You shall love your neighbor as yourself.'
There is no other commandment greater than these."*
Mark 12:30-31 (NKJV)

We are given a commandment from the Lord to love others as we love ourselves. A couple of days ago, I failed to do so.

I had been fighting a sinus infection. The extra pain, in addition to the discomfort I'd experienced every day for years, got to me. I was a mess. I didn't love myself very well. I looked in the mirror, discouraged by my appearance, and I hated what I saw.

Being sick on top of battling health issues is not a recipe for glamor. Feeling trapped in your body is very discouraging. I'm going to be honest with you, I gave in to the lies and the *what ifs*. I gave in to self-hate. I'm going to tell you the lies I fell for, because I know I'm not the only one who has heard the same whispers from the enemy. This is humbling for me to share, but I'm not trying to impress you. I'm hoping to remind you that you're not alone and encourage you to call out your own lies. So here we go:

"Kaitlyn, you're ugly. Your body has failed you. Look at so and so's body and how much stronger she is. Look how beautiful other women are compared to you. Kaitlyn, your husband would be happier with another woman, someone he didn't have to take care of so much. Kaitlyn, your kids deserve a normal mom, a mom who doesn't need to take naps. Kaitlyn, you'll never feel like yourself again. Kaitlyn, your life is awful. It's hopeless. God must not think you're worth healing. You'd bring more glory to God dead than alive. You should give up. You should quit praying for a miracle. You should stop writing a book. Actually, you should erase everything you've already written." And so on and so forth.

Do any of these lies sound familiar to you? The enemy was having a heyday with my thoughts, and I didn't fight like I should have. I see more clearly now. I was being attacked, and instead of holding up my shield of faith, I made myself defenseless. I became open to the affront.

I've felt so much guilt over the things I can't do, feeling like I'm holding my family back. It was a dark day, and I felt myself sinking. I reached out to my sisters and close friends, asking them for some back up. I was real, raw, and honest about everything I was thinking. We need people in our lives who can support us when we are messy, don't we? People who won't judge us in our weaknesses, but also won't let us stay there.

They all spoke truth into my situation—truth to my heart. They acknowledged the pain and didn't diminish its presence but reminded me better days would come.

My sister arrived at my front door with a card, bubble bath, and a beautiful bouquet of flowers. She reminded me I wasn't alone. My husband came home, and we wept together. He spoke the truth, and I listened. I told him my prayer that day was if God didn't intend to heal me, would He please take me home. Joel didn't like that, and he stopped me, cautioning to not put myself in the place of God. If He keeps me on earth, it's for a reason. Who am I to try and persuade Him otherwise?

Joel spoke to the guilt I felt. He reasoned with me, saying the guilt I deal with is over something I can't control. Through tears I told him he needs a healthy wife he can share adventures with. And through his own tears he replied, "I want you healthy, and I believe you will be. But even if things don't change, I want to do life with *you*. I made a vow to you, and you to me. And through sickness and health, for richer or poorer, for better or worse, *I do*."

As I already wrote about earlier, the devil has his tactics. One of them is guilt. He will try to make you feel badly about anything and everything to convince you that you're no longer a blessing, but rather a burden. That the world would be better off without you. I fell for it.

Thankfully, God is gracious and forgiving, and His mercies are new every morning. I went to sleep heavy-hearted but woke up feeling the freshness of a new day. His mercy at work in my life. I repented for allowing my tongue to be unbridled and my mind failing to take thoughts captive.

Some days are difficult, and others are worse. If you fail like I did on the harder days, just know that tomorrow is a new day, and there's new mercy for you in it.

There's a young woman who goes by the name of *Nightbirde* (her real name is Jane). She's been battling cancer for a long time. She's incredibly inspiring because she does an amazing job of choosing joy despite her circumstances. Something she wrote has stuck with me. "Don't you want to see what happens if you don't give up?" What a powerful question. Yes Jane, I do.

If you're like me, you're probably too critical of yourself. Would I expect from others what I expect from me? The answer is no. I got to thinking about how we are commanded to love others as we love ourselves. If a loved one was going through what I'm battling, I'd never want them to feel guilt over the things they couldn't do. Instead, I'd want them to know their life is valuable not because of what they do, but solely on who they are: human, a child of God, someone with a spirit, soul, and body.

Joel asked me what I would do if he became disabled. Would I wish to be with someone else? Would I be upset with him for things he could no longer achieve on his own? Would I hope he'd feel a sense of guilt over what he couldn't control? Of course not. Then why beat myself up over the same things I'd never shame anyone else for? I felt convicted. It was time to speak life over my body, so I did. "Body, you are strong. You're going to get through this. Good job! Body, you are healed. Kaitlyn, you are beautiful."

Let us never forget we are created in the image of God. So let's speak life over every part of us: our bodies, circumstances, finances, future, hopes, dreams, health, and more!

Proverbs 18:21 (NKJV) says, *"Death and life are in the power of the tongue, and those who love it will eat its fruit."* Your tongue, the words that you speak, bring life or death. Even on the hardest of days, I want to do better at speaking life. Who's with me?

COMPARISON IS THE THIEF OF JOY

I've never been one to compare myself to others, until the last couple of years. I never felt threatened by my gorgeous friends, never jealous of their beauty. I think that's why women's ministry was such a good fit for me. I just really loved the ladies and not once fell into the trap of comparison with them. I loved the differences. Red or blonde hair, full bodied or petite, loud or quiet, quirky or classy, I loved it all! But in this season of feeling limited and less than, I've found it much easier to wish I was someone else. I've wanted to have another person's body or be able to do what others can. And this is why I had to take a break from social media. It was not a trigger for me prior to my health challenges, but it became a source of pain and I needed to step away for a while. Going offline felt like a necessary boundary in my life.

As I already mentioned, for a long time I couldn't do much of anything with my kids. Remember, buttoning up their coats was difficult, let alone going on an amazing hike or jumping on a trampoline with them. And that's exactly what I saw scrolling through Instagram. I'd never wish what I'm going through on anyone, but it felt like other people's lives were moving forward while mine was stuck. And it was heartbreaking.

Social media increased the mom-guilt, wife-guilt, friend-guilt, look-good-feel-good-guilt, in my life. I wanted to go on ten mile runs in cute stretchy pants. I wanted to get dolled up and go out on the town with my man. I wanted to go on adventures! But these have had to wait.

I am so very thankful for high waisted pants. I need them in this season. They hold in what likes to hang out due to my lack of being able to exercise. Does anyone else appreciate the comeback of the old school pants? I share all this to say that I began to recognize I'd fallen into comparison, and it was leading me into guilt.

Social media can be really fun and good, but we have to remember it's just a small glimpse into people's lives. If you can't scroll without it making you feel sad about your own situation, or if it causes you to constantly compare, then take a step back from it. It's not worth it. In a lot of ways, it's a false reality, which is why I like to follow people who keep it real.

Be careful with your time and with your heart. If you need to unplug for a while like I did, that's okay. Actually, it's good to do. A lot of time is wasted scrolling through other people's lives, when that time could be spent in much better ways. President Theodore Roosevelt said, "Comparison is the thief of joy." He was right. I want to be known for joy, so I had better stop comparing.

1 Peter 1:3-9 talks about a joy so powerful it can't even be expressed! This is the joy I want to live with, and it comes from

knowing our inheritance through Christ Jesus. It doesn't come through life looking the way we had hoped. It's much deeper than that. *"Blessed be the God and Father of our Lord Jesus Christ, who according to His abundant mercy has begotten us again to a living hope through the resurrection of Jesus Christ from the dead, to an inheritance incorruptible and undefiled and that does not fade away, reserved in heaven for you, who are kept by the power of God through faith for salvation ready to be revealed in the last time. In this you greatly rejoice, though now for a little while, if need be, you have been grieved by various trials, that the genuineness of your faith, being much more precious than gold that perishes, though it is tested by fire, may be found to praise, honor, and glory at the revelation of Jesus Christ, whom having not seen you love. Though now you do not see Him, yet believing, you rejoice with joy inexpressible and full of glory, receiving the end of your faith—the salvation of your souls."* (NKJV)

Joy that lasts is not found in how we look or in what we can do. It's in the gift of salvation! We see in part right now, but a time is coming when we will be joined with our brothers and sisters in Christ, taking part in the marriage supper of The Lamb! Revelation 21:4 (NKJV) says, *"And God will wipe away every tear from their eyes; there shall be no more death, nor sorrow, nor crying. There shall there be no more pain, for the former things have passed away."*

Psalm 16:11 (NKJV) says joy is found in His presence! *"You will show me the path of life; in Your presence is fullness of joy; At Your right hand are pleasures forevermore."* I know this to be true because I am living it. I'm learning to walk through trials with joy. It is not easy, but it is possible.

We put a lot of emphasis on being happy in this world, thinking it comes from earthly treasure, like how much money we make, how good we look, or what things we get to do. But remember, Biblical happiness is so much deeper!

Oftentimes in the Bible, the word *blessed* actually means *happy*. Keeping that in mind, read James 1:12 (NIV) which says, *"Blessed (Happy) is the one who perseveres under trial because, having stood the test, that person will receive the crown of life that the Lord has promised to those who love him."* Come on! This is so encouraging. Happy is the man (or woman) who perseveres under trial!

What about the Beatitudes? Every time you read the word *blessed* in this passage, it means *happy*. I'm going to exchange those words in the text below, in hopes it will help you better understand where true happiness comes from.

Matthew 5:3–12 (NIV) Jesus said,

> *"Happy are the poor in spirit,*
> *for theirs is the kingdom of heaven.*
> *Happy are those who mourn,*
> *for they will be comforted.*
> *Happy are the meek,*
> *for they will inherit the earth.*
> *Happy are those who hunger and thirst for righteousness,*
> *for they will be filled.*
> *Happy are the merciful,*
> *for they will be shown mercy.*
> *Happy are the pure in heart,*
> *for they will see God.*
> *Happy are the peacemakers,*
> *for they will be called children of God.*
> *Happy are those who are persecuted because of righteousness,*
> *for theirs is the kingdom of heaven.*
> *Happy are you when people insult you, persecute you*
> *and falsely say all kinds of evil against you because of*
> *me. Rejoice and be glad, because great is your reward in*
> *heaven, for in the same way they persecuted the prophets*
> *who were before you."*

This passage of Scripture is both powerful and challenging. What a drastic difference in how God defines happiness and how the world does. I pray this revelation takes root in your heart today. I pray you will begin to walk in true happiness. Joy unspeakable and full of glory (1 Peter 1:8).

Joy is a third of the kingdom of heaven, according to Romans 14:17. Heaven is full of joy and full of those who have endured persecution and trial. They are now living in the reward given to those who persevere. May we learn to live in this kind of joy, experiencing true happiness, not based on our circumstances but on intimately knowing Jesus and our inheritance in Him.

Chapter 11

Jesus' Job Versus Our Job

Obedience paves the way for miracles!

As you read through the Bible, you'll notice healing came in many different ways. There was a specific purpose in the differences each time. Let's go through some of these stories and dig into the *whys* of them. I've touched on a few of these stories already, but let's take a closer look so we can better understand why God would heal one person one way, and another person in a different way.

God healed numerous people in the Old Testament, but I want to focus on the healings of Jesus that took place in the New Testament. I love reading about all the miracles Jesus did! My faith for the miraculous increases when I read the heart of Father God on display through the works of Jesus. He did so many that John 21:25 (NKJV) says, *"And there are also many other things which Jesus did, which if they were written one by one, I suppose that even the world itself could not contain the books that would be written."* What a statement! Jesus loves to heal, set captives free, and change people's lives for the best.

As we dig into a few of the miraculous works of Jesus, keep in mind we are only touching the surface of all the wonders He performed!

JAIRUS' DAUGHTER

Let's consider the healing of Jairus' daughter in Luke 8:40. Jairus was a ruler of the synagogue who found Jesus and fell at His feet, begging Him to come to his house because his only daughter (about twelve years old) was dying. Jesus responded by going with Jairus. But as He went, a crowd surrounded Him. This is when the woman with the issue of blood pressed through the crowd to receive her healing.

Luke 8:49–55 (NKJV) says, *"While He was still speaking* [to the woman with the issue of blood who had just received her healing], *someone came from the ruler of the synagogue's house, saying to him, 'Your daughter is dead. Do not trouble the Teacher.' But when Jesus heard it, He answered him, saying, 'Do not be afraid; only believe, and she will be made well.' When He came into the house, He permitted no one to go in except Peter, James, and John, and the father and mother of the girl. Now all wept and mourned for her; but He said, 'Do not weep; she is not dead, but sleeping.' And they ridiculed Him, knowing that she was dead. But He put them all outside, took her by the hand and called, saying, 'Little girl, arise.' Then her spirit returned, and she arose immediately. And He commanded that she be given something to eat."*

People ridiculed Jesus when He showed up to heal because they thought the situation was hopeless. The little girl was dead. Jesus' response to their ridicule was to put them all outside. Then, the miraculous took place. Their attitude did not stop Jesus or cause Him to doubt. I love that! He had them leave the house and did what He had come to do.

What do you do with distractions in your life? When the enemy comes at you with lies and confusion, do you allow him to stay, or do you remain focused on your God-given mission? The enemy will try to distract you with fear, doubt, and worry. He will mock your faith. and when you give in to those tactics, you will be weakened. But when you know the truth and keep your trust in the Lord, you will not be shaken. You will see the glory of God—the impossible made possible. This is where miracles take place.

Let this account be a reminder to take action against doubt so it doesn't control you. Put it, along with the doubters, outside. As you believe for healing, there will be those who ridicule you for it. They will think you're wrong for moving forward in faith. Let this story be a reminder to you that Jesus encountered doubters too. Instead of letting them get in His way, He put them outside and stayed focused on His purpose. Deal with doubt in your life. The same power that raised this little girl back to life and the same power that raised Jesus Himself back to life, lives in you (Romans 8:11).

PARALYTIC MAN

Now let's look at the story of the paralytic man who was lowered through the roof by his friends in order to get to Jesus. Luke 5:18-20 (NLT) says, *"Some men came carrying a paralyzed man on a sleeping mat. They tried to take him inside to Jesus, but they couldn't reach him because of the crowd. So they went up to the roof and took off some tiles. Then they lowered the sick man on his mat down into the crowd, right in front of Jesus. Seeing their faith, Jesus said to the man, 'Young man, your sins are forgiven.'"*

Seeing their faith. Whose faith was it? It was the faith of the *friends* that Jesus was referring to. Isn't it amazing these friends were willing to carry this man, remove tiles from a roof, and lower him down in the midst of a crowd, because they knew with certainty Jesus was able to heal? This story encourages me to stand in faith for others, to not give up believing for their miracle, and to help them get closer to Jesus. I hope it encourages you too.

When I read the Bible, I like to think about the reason certain passages were included. We know *"All Scripture is God-breathed and is useful for teaching, rebuking, correcting and training in righteousness, so that the servant of God may be thoroughly equipped for every good work,"* according to 2 Timothy 3:16–17 (NIV). So, if it's in the Word, there's a good reason for it.

The story found in Luke 5 is an encouragement to us to be friends of faith. Let's choose to come to the aid of those around us who lack strength and ability to stand on their own and help them get closer to Jesus—closer to their miracle. It's also a reminder that our healing doesn't solely depend on our faith for it. Has anyone ever told you you're not healed because you don't have enough faith? Unfortunately, it happens a lot. But the Bible says all you need is faith the size of a mustard seed to move mountains, and as shown in the paralytic's story, it was the faith of his friends that led to his healing.

If you're praying for a friend or family member's miracle, be encouraged by this story. Your faith for others can bring about the healing they long for. I'm more determined now than ever to pray for miracles. As I've mentioned before, my children and I pray for them every single night. And we won't stop. We've seen prayers answered, miracles coming to pass. Your faith for others is a gift.

Someone's healing could require *just* your prayers, or it might mean you need to act in faith like the friends in this story. It could involve you removing tiles from a roof, providing a rope, or working to get those in need to Jesus. If that's the kind of friend you want to be, isn't it worth it? Of course it is!

WOMAN WITH THE ISSUE OF BLOOD

Earlier, we looked at the story of the woman with the issue of blood, but we are going to spend a little time going through her story here as well.

Remember Jesus didn't go to the woman. The woman went to Him. She broke the cultural rules and pressed through a crowd of people so she could touch the hem of His garment. It was her desperation to get to Jesus and her determination to touch Him that led to her healing.

Why would this story be included in the Bible? I see so many reasons, but one is to encourage us to pursue the Lord, seeking Him and pressing through anything trying to hold us back from getting to Him. She could have allowed the embarrassment of her condition (continuous vaginal bleeding) to keep her home. But instead, she conquered fear, moving forward in spite of it.

"Courage isn't the absence of fear, but rather the assessment that something is more important than fear."
- Franklin D. Roosevelt

Courage is doing something when you're afraid. I wonder what she thought as she headed out the door that day. She knew Jesus was coming, so she stepped out of her home and into the crowd, despite the fear of what others would think. Mark 5:33 (NKJV) says, *"But the woman, fearing and trembling, knowing what had happened to her, came and fell down before Him and told Him the whole truth."* According to the laws of the day, she was not supposed to be out in public because her condition deemed her *unclean.* She was fully aware, but also resolved to not allow fear to stop her from pursuing Jesus for healing.

It's one thing to experience fear and another to allow it to control you. God has not given us a spirit of fear, according to 2 Timothy 1:7. There is no fear in love, for perfect love drives it away, says 1 John 4:18. So if you're experiencing fear, it means a part of you is not operating in the love of God.

The woman with the issue of blood trembled before Jesus, knowing she had just been healed by touching the hem of His garment. His words to her dispelled fear, for He spoke courage over her. His power healed her, and His love drove fear away. If you walk in fear, make it your daily prayer to experience God's love. Fear won't last when His love takes over.

It's also important to recognize she had suffered for twelve years, yet she did not give up. She had the will to live and the drive to pursue healing. Twelve years of continuously bleeding would be incredibly discouraging, painful, messy, and exhausting. It was also costly. She had spent all the money she had on physicians. But instead of getting better, she got worse, until Jesus came to town, that is.

Let her story encourage you to never give up. Let it be a reminder to live with hope, no matter what! This woman had enough hope left in her to get out of bed, out of her house, and through a crowd, to reach Jesus. She pressed through the people who surrounded Him, getting low enough to touch his hem. In that moment, she knew she chose rightly to live with hope! She knew her life was worth fighting for. And friend, your life is too!

Another incredible part of this story is that Jesus took the time to speak to her when He could have easily continued on His way. She received healing. He not only wanted her to be healed, but He also wanted her restored. Jesus knew fear was present, and He addressed it. He knew she had been an outcast and in front of everyone, He declared her whole. She was no longer to be considered cursed and unclean.

He not only wants us healed, but He also wants us to be set free from everything that hinders us from living an abundant life in Him. Today, Jesus wants to remind you you're worth His time. He is not too busy for you. Maybe you need to learn from this woman's example of stepping out of a comfort zone and move towards Jesus. If she could do it, so can you. She is one of the top ten people I'm looking forward to meeting in heaven. What an incredible inspiration to me!

BLIND MAN

In so many other accounts of healing, an action is required of the person Jesus is ministering to. John 9 tells the story of the man born blind. After Jesus made a mixture of His spit and dirt, He put it on the blind man's eyes and told him to go and wash in the pool of Siloam. The man obeyed and came back seeing!

LAZARUS

Lazarus was obedient from the grave. Jesus called out to him saying, "Lazarus come forth!" And he did as Jesus commanded (John 11:43).

INVALID AT POOL OF BETHESDA

What about the man who had been an invalid for thirty-eight years, lying by the pool of Bethesda? His story is found in John 5. John 5:6-7 (NIV) reads *"When Jesus saw him lying there and learned that he had been in this condition for a long time, he asked him, 'Do you want to get well?' 'Sir,' the invalid replied, 'I have no one to help me into the pool when the water is stirred. While I am trying to get in, someone else goes down ahead of me.'"* But Jesus! He was about to give this man a command that would transform his life. In verse 8 Jesus replied, *"'Get up! Pick up your mat and walk.' At once the man was cured; he picked up his mat and walked."* The man obeyed Jesus, and because he did, he was miraculously healed!

It's Jesus' job to heal. Our job is to obey Him. What is He asking you to do? What word has He spoken that you've ignored? It's time for you to obey the word of the Lord.

Healing is not a *one size fits all*. What is consistent in the stories of healing in the Bible is an action step of obedience to Jesus for healings to come to pass. Think about it. People were told to come forth, go in faith, go and wash, pick up your mat, rise up, etc. I don't agree with theology that says healing is solely dependent on our faith. But I do believe our obedience to the voice of Jesus is crucial for it to come to pass. Obedience paves the way for miracles. Don't ignore His voice, for in it is your victory.

Obedience paves the way for miracles!

Chapter 12

Where I Am Now

"Do not sorrow, for the joy of the Lord is your strength."
Nehemiah 8:10b (NKJV)

I've gotten through the worst of it. The season of needing 24/7 help is over. I've been able to clean my own toilets for months now. Even though it's not my favorite thing to do, I'm thankful for the ability to do it. Being sick makes you appreciate feeling good. You don't realize what you take for granted until you're no longer able to do simple tasks like taking showers or folding laundry. When you don't feel well, you dream of all the things you hope to do one day. And you recognize you held back on adventures you could have taken when you felt healthy.

I have told Joel that once I'm healed, we need to plan a trip to Alaska for the fishing trip of his dreams! You go out into the wilderness for a week, fly fish all day, then sleep in a tent. I can't wait! I'm ready to make that memory with my man!

Before this health battle, I was hesitant to make this kind of plan. Could I leave the kids for a week? Would it be too rough and tough in a tent for that long? Maybe we should stay at a resort and go for the more glamorous experience of wild salmon Alaska fishing. But now I'm itching for that type of adventure! The day I'm healed, I think we should buy the tickets!

Overall, I'm doing better, yet I'm still experiencing tiring symptoms all day, every day. My vision has continued to be an issue. It's hard to explain. I can see clearly, yet it doesn't feel right yet. It's hard to look far away, and often feels difficult to look further than just a couple of feet away. Again, it's hard to explain. I still have constant nerve sensitivity, especially in my mouth. Oftentimes my tongue feels like it's being blowtorched, but sometimes the rest of my face does too. It seems as if I'm moving when in reality, I am not. Just imagine feeling like you're constantly on a boat or walking on waves. Many times I feel I'm going to tip over, and that, my friends, is not a fun feeling. These are the main symptoms. The minor ones are tightness in my jaw, headaches, fatigue, and weird sensations on my face.

Why do I share this with you? Going back and reading through it, I realize it sounds sad. But I want you to know about these struggles, because I'm still holding on to hope. I'm still pressing through and living life. No matter what you're going through, you can live with hope too. I could easily call it quits and give up believing for my healing. I could allow sorrow to take over and become depressed. I could find an unhealthy way to cope with the battle. But ultimately my strength comes from the Lord!

Lately, as I've thought about all I go through on a daily basis, I've begun to realize I really am strong. It's not because I'm awesome, it's because God's Word is true. In 2 Corinthians 12:9 (NKJV) it says, *"And He said to me, 'My grace is sufficient for you, for My strength is made perfect in weakness. Therefore most gladly I will rather boast in my infirmities, that the power of Christ may rest upon me.'"*

The strength I'm walking in comes from the Lord. What a gift it is! I've said this many times, and I mean it, "I don't know how I would get through this without Jesus." This doesn't mean I'm always strong. Oh no. I still struggle plenty, but I 100 percent believe God is walking with me and getting me through this trial. I still have days where I feel depleted and weary, but on those days, I have a stronger inner knowing that better days will come. Despair is not winning. Most days I'm choosing joy.

I've always admired the Apostle Paul's ability to write about joy when he was in prison. I've been encouraged by the obedience of Abraham, that he was willing to sacrifice his long-awaited son, Isaac, on the altar (thankful God provided a ram instead). I've loved the courage of Queen Esther. She was willing to die in order to save others. She moved forward despite fear. The heroes of the faith are recorded as such because their relationship with God, and their trust in Him, was notable.

From a young age, I've wanted to walk in faith, trust, joy, and courage like the Bible characters I've spent my life reading about. And then this season came, and with it an opportunity to live with hope when others would more easily despair. Some have told me I've been *entrusted* with this hardship. That God is trusting me to walk it out well. It doesn't make life easier, but it does put my trial into perspective.

When I read about the heroes of the faith, do you know what I see in them? I see the ability to walk out suffering and hardship while choosing to trust God no matter what. I see them choosing to rejoice in hope despite their circumstances. They lived through their trial well, and I want to do the same.

I would rather live my life as a woman of faith, no matter how I feel, than to fill my days with sorrow. I believe enduring the battle I'm in *well* looks like waking up each morning declaring the goodness of God, contending in faith for my miracle throughout the day, and going to bed giving thanks for His faithfulness each night. I have so much to be thankful for, even when I don't feel good.

EVEN IF INSTEAD OF *WHAT IF*

Too often we entertain the *what ifs* instead of declaring *even if* and *no matter what*. These *what-ifs* usually hold an element of fear. But when we can say, *"Even if*, Lord, You will take care of me,"* or *"No matter what*, I trust Your plan"* then we move away from fear and closer to trust.

Recently I had an appointment at a new doctor's office and saw a physician's assistant there. She ordered an MRI of my jugular veins, which revealed elevated vascular pressure in them. She told me she was 98 percent sure I had something called Eagle's syndrome. That's when your styloid bones move, oftentimes due to trauma, and infringe on the veins. In my case, she suspected the infringement was also impacting my nerves as well.

The cure? Surgery. It was a lot to take in, but I was thankful for an answer. Finally, a professional told me something to explain what's been going on in my body, after years of trying to figure it out. A CTV of my neck and head was ordered for further clarity on the issue.

I had a follow up appointment to go over the results and learned the scan did not confirm Eagle's syndrome. Instead, I was told we still needed to figure out where the vascular pressure was coming from because my styloid bones were not infringing the way they had suspected. So, an additional test, called a venogram, was ordered. They go through your groin, insert a catheter, and use a tube that goes through your vein to measure the pressure between your heart and head.

What was my response to this news? I wept. I wept a lot. What I thought was an answer actually led to more questions. After getting out a big ole' cry, I surrendered it all to the Lord again. My heart let out, "I trust you God. You will heal me." And then I worshiped Him. My day was not ruined. I still had reason to give thanks.

Joel came home expecting to find me sad. So when he asked me how I was and I responded with, "I'm good," he was surprised. I told him at this point, I'm left with only two options. I could either trust God or not, and I choose to trust Him. Spending time in worship shifted the atmosphere of disappointment into one of peace that passes understanding.

It's called a sacrifice of praise for a reason. When we want to crawl into bed and cry the day away is when it's time to offer up a sacrifice of thanksgiving and praise. When we do this, it shifts our perspective and realigns us with God's heart. Even more, we show the world what breakthrough and victory looks like. Choosing to trust the Lord despite uncertainty and pain is breakthrough.

The same is true for you. If you're facing uncertainty of any kind, perhaps your finances are dwindling, your relationships are suffering, your child has backslidden, or your body is hurting... your ability to turn your eyes upon Jesus and declare your trust in Him is evidence of breakthrough.

You are victorious, my friend. You show that victory when you choose joy, when you open your mouth in praise, when you speak blessing instead of cursing, and when you pray instead of complaining. When you testify of God's goodness instead of focusing on everything going wrong in your life you are victorious. Keep going!

KEEP LOOKING HEAVENWARD

The song from *Charlotte's Web*, "Chin Up," just popped in my head and the lyrics are applicable to my life right now. I'm going to share them with you!

Chin up, chin up, everybody loves a happy face
Wear it, share it, it'll brighten up the darkest place
Twinkle, sparkle, let a little sunshine in

You'll be on the right side, looking at the bright side up with
your chinny chin chin...
Chin up, chin up, put a little laughter in your eyes
Brave it, save it, even though you're feeling otherwise
Rise up, wise up, make a little smile begin
You'll be happy hearted, once you get it started
Up with your chinny chin chin!
Chin down, you can't come frowning
Turn around, starting, clowning
Think sad, your troubles double
Think glad, they burst like bubbles
Chin up, chin up, every little time your spirit's wilt
Chin up, chin up, give your attitude an upward tilt
Twinkle, sparkle, make a little fun begin
You'll be on the right side, looking at the bright side
Up with your chinny chin, chin up!

Chin up, my friend! You are going to make it! Heaven is cheering you on and I am too. More breakthroughs are coming. As you go about your day or get out of bed tomorrow morning, I want you to realize you are walking in breakthrough.

Choosing to get up is breakthrough. Getting ready and putting on the armor of God is breakthrough. Opening your mouth in praise and thanksgiving is breakthrough. Remember, every breath you take is breakthrough! You can do this, my friend!

Although more healing needs to take place, I look back and realize how far I've come. The picture on the left was taken at my sickest. The picture on the right was taken two years later. It's good to remember how God has carried me through the hardest days.

At this point, I'm left with only two options:
to either trust God or not, and I choose to trust Him.

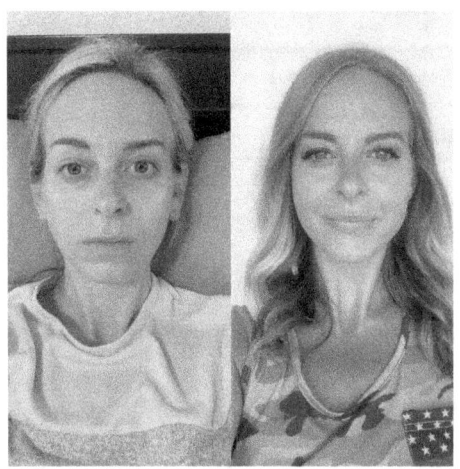

It's good to remember how far God has brought me.

A moment when I was at my sickest.
My sweet Esther crawled up on my lap to comfort me.

Chapter 13

Give Thanks

"Rejoice always, pray without ceasing, in everything give thanks; for this is the will of God in Christ Jesus for you."
1 Thessalonians 5:16-18 (NKJV)

I've said it before, and I'll say it again: we have so much to be thankful for! The more I focus on where I can give thanks, the more joy I walk in and release to others. The Bible says a merry heart does good like medicine (Proverbs 17:22). So that means a glad heart, a joyful heart, is like medicine. That is so powerful. When our hearts choose joy, our bodies are nourished.

As I get better, but still struggle, I'm working on giving thanks for the seemingly small things. But truth be told, they're really the most important things. The pen marks on my cabinets, random toys in random places, crumbs and dirty floors. I've found myself grateful for them. Why? Because the messes are evidence that little ones are in my home. It's evidence of their precious lives. This applies to my husband too. I'm thankful for the scrambled egg mess on the counter every morning and the never-ending laundry, because it means I still have him. The evidence of life should not be a burden, but rather a reason to give thanks.

The evidence of life should not be a burden,
but rather a reason to give thanks.

Years ago, I was in a rush to leave the house to get the kids to school and myself to work. I was stressed out and my little one would not get her socks and shoes on quickly enough. If you've ever had to leave the house with a kid in tow, you've probably encountered the same struggle. The one where it takes them about thirty minutes to put their socks and shoes on. Am I right? Why, oh why, oh Lord, lol! I started raising my voice saying, "Get your socks on now! Come on! Hurry up!" And then I felt the Holy Spirit stop me in my tracks, right there in my garage. He whispered to me, "Would you want it any other way?" And I knew what He meant.

Would I rather *not* have kids and *not* be stressed about them finding their socks and shoes? I felt His sweet conviction in such a strong way. It was powerful and beautiful. And my answer was, "Of course not." I'd take the stress and mess of having kids any day versus not having them in my life. My attitude shifted. I became grateful in that moment. *Thank you, God, that I have a daughter! Thank you, God, that she's healthy and able to find her own socks and shoes.*

I know that being a parent has its moments of stress. But when we switch our mindset from one of negativity to positivity, it will change us and those around us for the better. Look for the good. Look for the reasons to be thankful in your life. You won't regret it. Finding gratitude in the small things will help sustain you in the big things, like when you're clinging to hope for healing.

I am not perfect at this, but I can say that I'm pretty good at it. I'm genuinely thankful for the evidence of having children and a husband in my home. One day there won't be as many handprints on the glass, or toothpaste smeared on the bathroom vanity. One day I won't find smashed goldfish in every crevice of my car or have Legos to trip over. There won't be fifteen loads of laundry to do every week, crumbs on every chair and underneath my table, or a pile of shoes by the door. One day I won't be interrupted while using the bathroom and I'll be able to get ready in silence. I won't find streaks of markers on my walls or have to break up a fight because little sister bit big sister. I tear up as I write this because I know I will miss those things. I will miss the craziness of it all!

My little girl woke me up at five thirty this morning saying, "Mom, I pooped my pants." She was lying in our bed as she said this, by the way. And she had, in fact, pooped her pants. I took her to the bathroom and helped clean her up, and as I did, she said, "I'm sorry, mom." I told her she didn't have anything to be sorry about. It happens. I've pooped my pants too. And in that moment, I was thankful I was able to get up, walk, and help my little girl. That might sound like a silly example, but it's true. I'm choosing to find the reasons to give thanks. And it's powerful.

A couple of days ago, that same little girl got car sick and missed the bowl. I got out the baby wipes and went to work. As I cleaned up the puddle of puke, I realized I was thankful in that moment too. Not because she got sick, but because I was able to clean it up. A couple of years ago I would have lacked strength for the task. Who would've thought I'd be happy to clean up vomit? But in all honesty, I was. Every time I clean my toilets, I'm thankful. Any task that required bending over used to be difficult for me. So now that I am able to, I'm thankful.

---

*"This is the day that the Lord has made;
we will rejoice and be glad in it." Psalm 118:24 (NKJV)*

Are you finding reasons to rejoice today? If you are struggling to do so, simply acknowledge that the Lord made this day, and thank Him for it. I know from experience it's not always easy to find things to rejoice about. On the harder days, I have to work a little more at being thankful. But I've always had an opportunity to give thanks. The sun has risen every morning. I've never gone without food. I have suffered, but I've always been in a warm home. My kids are still thriving. My husband still loves me. And God has always been with me. It's possible to give thanks, even when the pain feels over-whelming.

Consider this truth: it's God's will for us to give thanks without condition. In 1 Thessalonians 5:16–18 (NKJV), we're told to, *"Rejoice always, pray without ceasing, in everything give thanks; for this is the will of God in Christ Jesus for you."* Did you catch that? The verse says that in *everything*, give thanks. Why? Because thanks-giving will increase joy in your life, and therefore offer nourishment to your body and medicine for your soul!

The Apostle Paul wrote what is said to be *Paul's joy letter* (the book of Philippians) from prison. I want to highlight a few of the verses he wrote, not from the comfort of his home as I am writing now, but while he was under arrest for preaching about Jesus:

> *"But what things were gain to me, these I have counted loss for Christ. Yet indeed I also count all things loss for the excellence of the knowledge of Christ Jesus my Lord, for whom I have suf-fered the loss of all things, and count them as rubbish, that I may gain Christ."*
> (Philippians 3:7–8 NKJV)

> *"Rejoice in the Lord always. Again I will say, rejoice!"*
> (Philippians 4:4 NKJV)

> *"I have learned in whatever state I am, to be content."*
> (Philippians 4:11b NKJV)

> *"I can do all things through Christ who strengthens me."*
> (Philippians 4:13 NKJV)

Friends, think about the setting Paul was in as he wrote. He had learned to be content, even while unjustly bound. I appreciate that about him because being content doesn't always come naturally for us. But we can still be encouraged in knowing it's something that can be learned.

Just as a reminder, Paul was beaten and stoned, shipwrecked, persecuted, imprisoned, and rejected. He had endured so much he thought he'd never survive. In 2 Corinthians 1:8-9 (NKJV) he writes, *"For we do not want you to be ignorant, brethren, of our trouble which came to us in Asia: that we were burdened beyond measure, above strength, so that we despaired even of life. Yes, we had the sentence of death in ourselves, that we should not trust in ourselves but in God who raises the dead."* Through despairing times, he continued to trust the Lord!

His entire world changed after his encounter with God. Paul could have complained about his trials, comparing what his life once looked like to all he was going through after his salvation. He could have gone to the Lord confused about what had seemingly gone wrong. But instead, Paul said the things that once were valuable to him, he now counted as worthless compared to the value of knowing Jesus. Christ became worth it all—worth his job, home, friends, position, influence, and comfort. He lived for something greater than himself. And as he did, he learned to be content no matter what.

It's easy to read through the writings of Paul and forget where he was when he wrote them. From this point on, please keep in mind that Paul wrote about joy *from a prison cell.* Joy is not based on circumstances. If it was, he would have been full of sorrow. Joy comes when we choose to give thanks in *all* things and keep our focus heavenward.

If you knew taking a vitamin would benefit your body, and it was available to you at any given time, wouldn't you take it? Of course you would! In the same way, thanksgiving and joy are available to you always, and they will benefit your spirit, soul, and body. I'm no doctor, but I'd say that it's worth trying.

A great exercise to develop thankfulness in your life is to think about the things that make you smile and write them down. I think of it like strengthening a muscle. In order to do so, you have to work out, lift weights on a regular basis, go on a bike ride a few times a week, go swimming, etc. You won't develop muscles by working out only one time. But you will if you're consistent and intentional about it. The same is true of building what I like to call your *joy muscle* or *thankfulness muscle*.

Fourteen years ago I started a *Things to Smile About* journal. In it are listed over a thousand things that bring me joy. When I was in the habit of writing in it frequently, I found I was always looking for what brought me life. In doing so, the world was a pretty bright place!

I have my children write down three things a day they are thankful for. We've missed a few days, but that's okay. It's incredible to see what they come up with. Even my five-year-old, Esther, is amazing at finding joy in her life! If you have kiddos, I'd encourage you to do this with them!

To give you a some ideas, a few of the things written in my joy journal are: sunrises, oatmeal, baths, pianos, worship songs, comfortable pj's, spinach pie, butterflies, non-toxic candles, bald eagles, cheese, snail mail, wildflowers, paths made by deer, lipstick, shooting stars, dark chocolate, kombucha, bubble gum, rainbows, weddings, an anointed violinist, elderly couples still in love and not afraid to show it, caramel popcorn mixed with white cheddar popcorn, Dad's hard work, Mom's zeal for the Lord, toads, honesty, bravery, freedom, a light breeze, my hammock, chocolate fondue, hiking, people watching, adoption stories, freckles, the smell of freshly brewed coffee in the morning (and the first sip of it), meadowlarks, and traveling.

It is fun to think about all the little things that put a smile on my face. It's also a fun way to get to know yourself and others. I love knowing what brings people joy and the quirks that make them unique. Some of you might be delighted by a Reuben sandwich. If you were my friend, I'd want to know that, because I'd love to randomly bring you one for lunch someday! P.S. I love Reubens!

When you have your list, and want to share it, I'd love to see what makes you smile too.

The more aware you are of all that is good, the more thankful you will become. It's a beautiful cycle that goes like this:

Look for the good ➞ the more thankful you'll become
➞ the happier you will be ➞ the healthier you'll become
➞ the more thankful you'll be!

"I will give thanks and praise You, O Lord my God, with all my heart; And will glorify Your name forevermore" Psalm 86:12 (AMP). May it be said of us that we give thanks to God and praise Him with *all* of our hearts! May our whole heart glorify His name forever!

Use the following space to write down things that make you smile, and/or things you are thankful for. Remember, it can be something as small as a snowflake or as momentous as getting to watch the birth of a baby:

....

....

....

....

....

....

....

Chapter 14

Our Thoughts Matter

*"Finally, brothers and sisters, whatever is true,
whatever is noble, whatever is right, whatever is pure,
whatever is lovely, whatever is admirable—if anything is
excellent or praiseworthy—think about such things."*
Philippians 4:8 (NIV)

WHAT IFS AREN'T TRUTHS

I remember a time many years ago when I was consistently entertaining *what if* scenarios and hopping on their *what if* trains.
Were these producing hope and positivity in my life? No, they were
always worst-case scenarios that led to fear and worry. I'm not
proud I allowed my mind to wander, or that I engaged the thoughts
instead of taking them captive. But I'm sharing this because the
Holy Spirit taught me a valuable lesson during, and I believe He
wants you to learn from my mistakes.

Have you ever let thoughts develop into worst-case scenarios
and play out a terrible *what if* story in your mind? Once I became a
mom, I feared what could happen to my kids if I wasn't always with
them. The worry only increased when I played *what if* scenarios in

my mind. There was a period of time I didn't like driving because of irrational fear. *What if* a tire blew? *What if* another car crashed into mine? When I got sick, I started thinking *what if* I never get better? *What if* there's a tumor on my brain? *What if* I'll never feel normal again? *What if* the best is behind me? Am I the only one who has done this? It would be amazing if so, but I doubt I am. Why do we think up terrible outcomes in our minds and then wonder why we struggle with fear?

Maybe you have been doing this for a long time, and don't know how to stop. No judgment here, I get it. But it's good to ask ourselves why we entertain fear. Why do we allow our minds to play out a horror story that produces bondage in our lives? It's a tactic of the enemy to go after our thoughts, but we can't blame the devil when we indulge those thoughts by keeping them going. We have been given the ability to take every thought captive and make it obedient to Christ (2 Corinthians 10:5). So the question is, will we use our God-given authority or not?

I don't know how long I'd been hopping on the *what if* trains, but the Holy Spirit was gracious to confront me about it. I was reading Philippians 4:8 one day, when it was as if the words leapt off the page. God's dividing sword of truth penetrated my heart. "Whatever is true, think about such things" were highlighted to me and the Holy Spirit spoke: *"What ifs aren't truths."* Boom! A truth bomb was dropped!

Every time I focused on a *what if*, I wasn't thinking on things that were... *true*. While the *what ifs* felt real, like things that could and would happen, they hadn't happened. I was literally entertaining lies. And if truth sets us free (John 8:32) then lies bind us up. I could no longer justify entertaining the *what ifs* and playing out worst-case scenarios.

The next time a *what if* train came steaming by, I used my God-given authority to stop it instead of hopping onto it. That simple act of obedience began to transform my life!

In 2 Timothy 1:7 (NKJV), it says, *"For God has not given us a spirit of fear, but of power and of love and of a sound mind."* Fear is not from God. Therefore, thoughts that provoke fear aren't either. What is from God though, is a sound mind. And in this verse, a sound mind means self-control. We are given self-control, which allows us to stop our thoughts from wandering into despair and choosing what we focus on instead. And as my dear friend, Miss Judy, often says, *what we focus on we give power to.*

CHOOSE WISELY

The other day I felt God speaking to my heart. He said, "You choose what you fear." So if I choose to entertain thoughts that aren't in line with His Word, and if that thought provokes fear, the fault lies with me. If I'm constantly fearing I'll never feel normal again, it's because I haven't come into agreement with Isaiah 53:5 that says I am healed by the stripes of Jesus. Friend, we have the power to stop fear by taking thoughts captive and declaring truth. My thoughts matter. Your thoughts matter too.

Peace is the result of thinking on things that are true, noble, right, pure, lovely, and admirable. Philippians 4:9 (NKJV) says, *"The things which you learned and received and heard and saw in me, these do, and the God of peace will be with you."* Isaiah 26:3 (NKJV) says, *"You will keep him in perfect peace, whose mind is stayed on You, because he trusts in You."* The word *mind* in this verse is the Hebrew word *yeser,* and part of its meaning is as follows: *of what is framed in the mind, imagination, device, and purpose.* The things we imagine need to be in line with the Word of God, not subjected to the enemy's lies.

It's time to stop the negative *what if* trains. The next time you start to entertain worst case scenarios or ride *what if* trains, picture yourself pulling the brake and bringing it to a stop. You can do it! You've been given the power and authority in Jesus' name to take every thought captive and make it obedient to Jesus.

God knows and cares about our thoughts, so let's live in ways they honor Him. Think about how much better our lives would be if we lived not only doing what we know is right but thinking on the right things too. Many times in the Bible, we learn Jesus perceived people's thoughts and knew what they were thinking. Let this put a holy fear of the Lord in us. We may fail, but it doesn't mean we should quit trying to honor Him in every way, including what goes through our minds.

Our walk with the Lord is a continuous journey of becoming more like Him. He is gracious with us and knows we aren't perfect, yet He desires we are holy, as He is holy (1 Peter 1:16). The more we *think* like Him, the more we will *be* like Him.

In 2 Corinthians 3:18 (AMP), it says, *"And we all, with unveiled face, continually seeing as in a mirror the glory of the Lord, are progressively being transformed into His image from [one degree of] glory to [even more] glory, which comes from the Lord, [who is] the Spirit."* I love this! We are progressively being transformed into His image. It takes time, but what an encouragement to know He is changing us so we're more like Him.

TRANSFORMATION IS WORTH THE INVESTMENT

Transformation comes from the renewing of our minds. As Romans 12:2 (AMP) says, *"And do not be conformed to this world [any longer with its superficial values and customs], but be transformed and progressively changed [as you mature spiritually] by the renewing of your mind [focusing on godly values and ethical attitudes], so that you may prove [for yourselves] what the will of God is, that which is good and acceptable and perfect [in His plan and pur-pose for you]."*

You might be wondering, "How do I renew my mind?" It's a good question to ask. In Romans 12:2, the word *renewal* is the Greek word *anakainōsis* and it means a renewal, renovation, and com-plete change for the better.

If you've ever gone through a home renovation, you know it requires time, planning, and hard work. Unless something went terribly wrong, you'd probably agree it all paid off when the outcome was just what you wanted. Renovations don't happen quickly, but the process is worth the time they take to make happen.

Have you ever heard it said *there's purpose in the pain, purpose in the process?* Easier to say than to live out, but I believe these statements to be true. I've wrestled with understanding the purpose of God's timing for my healing. I've had a hard time seeing the point in it taking so long, but I know that God is working. He is making renovations in my heart and soul. He's changing me for the better. I believe He has a plan and is allowing the suffering to continue for a reason. Sometimes I weep as I declare my continued faith for healing, but I trust Him, nonetheless.

I recognize that good things often take time to come to pass. Growth requires time. It takes nine months for a baby to develop in the womb. It takes a season for a seed to sprout, and even longer for it to bloom. If you try to rush the necessary timing, you'll miss out on the harvest it would have provided. A garden takes hard work and a lot of time. But the benefit of going through the process is worth it in the end.

Allow the Lord to renew and renovate you. If there's anything you are holding back from Him, surrender it today. If you feel trapped in addiction, bound by harassing thoughts, weighed down by sorrow, spend time with God. Open your Bible and meditate on His Word. Turn on worship music. Ask the Lord for renewal and transformation in your life. Give Him permission to renovate the areas that need a complete change for the better. Don't give up in the process of being renewed. No matter how long it takes, remember that it is worth it.

When I finally stopped the wrong trains of thought and instead focused on truth, it helped transform my mind. A bad habit was conquered, making way for a healthy one. That is renewal. And it came through revelation I received while reading the Word, then applying it in my life.

The Word reveals God's heart. When we know it, we have a point of reference for what our behaviors, thoughts, emotions, and attitudes should be. Our minds become renewed as we live by His Word. Is it always easy? No. But it is possible. Will we fail? Probably. But we will get better as we walk it out daily and contend for it through prayer.

Contend means to struggle and surmount. Renewal of your mind means you must put in the work. It might be a real challenge, but you will find victory if you don't give up or give in. It's worth fighting for, though, because the renewing of your mind brings transformation in your life.

Think about it this way. If you knew someone hated you and was trying to destroy your life, would you sit back or fight back? Keeping that in mind, consider that the enemy of your soul is hoping to derail your thought-life every day. Because he's the Father of Lies, he's good at it. But as a believer, you can fight back with Truth and stand victorious.

In bed this morning I got a picture of Superman and the many times he flew to those in danger. I pictured him coming to the rescue of hundreds of people on a train that was about to be derailed. He got there just in time, and using his super strength pushed against the front of the train, bringing it to a stop.

Because of Jesus, you have supernatural strength inside of you. You have the ability to stop trains. The next time you get derailed in your thoughts or hop on the wrong train, remember the strength of God is living inside you. Bring the train to a stop and get it back on the right track.

Matthew 22:37 (NIV) says, *"Jesus replied: 'Love the Lord your God with all your heart and with all your soul and with all your mind.'"* What a good reminder to love God with our thoughts. And not just some of them, but all of them. This might feel daunting, but it can happen through the renewal process.

OURS TO PROTECT

God has been so faithful to me in this season while writing this book. Just when I think I've run out of content, He's there telling me what to write about next. He showed me three areas we need to protect for our thoughts to be honoring to Him. He's shown me over and over throughout this journey, that He's not just interested in me being healthy physically. He wants my soul (my mind, will, and emotions) healthy too. A big part of having a healthy mind is through having healthy thoughts. Let's unpack the areas God highlighted to me, together.

WHAT WE LISTEN TO

I like to spend a lot of time listening to worship music. It fills my home and car almost every day. I've found the songs I have on repeat are the same ones running through my mind in the middle of the night. They're also the words I sing first thing in the morning.

I've taken note of it, especially when I've woken up during the night with such powerful lyrics running through my mind. My spirit is being ministered to as I sleep. And it's a result of filling up on things that are true, noble, right, pure, lovely, and admirable during the day. It's made me want to continue saturating myself in worship, as well as soaking my home, children, and husband in it. Because as we know, the truth will set us free. And as we hear it being declared, God's promises take root in our heart and renews us in Him.

WHAT WE WATCH

Have you ever awakened from a terrible dream and wondered why on earth you had a nightmare, only to remember that you watched a scary movie the night before? Or if you or someone you love has struggled with pornography, then you know those images deeply affect the brain and cause immoral thoughts. No doubt what we watch will affect our thoughts.

Not too long ago, I was watching a show I'd recently started and watched more than I should have. At first, I tried to justify why I thought it was ok. But the more I watched the more defiled I felt. I knew I needed to turn it off and had no regrets once I did.

If you're watching something that calls evil good and good evil, I encourage you to ask yourself, "Why am I justifying this? Is it worth it?" Is entertainment more important than righteous living? I've never regretted the times that I followed the conviction of the Holy Spirit. He wants what's best for us. He knows what will tear us down and what will call us up higher. Remember, His "no" means a better "yes."

God is gracious and doesn't deal with all of our issues at once (thankfully). Maybe you haven't felt convicted about the things you watch, and if that's the case, I encourage you to ask the Lord for a greater level of discernment. Ask Him to increase your love for what is good and your hatred for what is evil. Honestly, we should all be praying for this on a regular basis. And then, when you feel His conviction, respond in obedience. And I daresay you won't regret it either.

How does social media affect your thoughts? I've previously shared the necessary boundaries I took to keep me focused on healing rather than everyone else's seemingly blissful lives. But I'd also like to encourage you here to get offline if it's negatively affecting your thoughts.

In Deuteronomy 5 we find the Ten Commandments listed. Verse 21 (NKJV) says, *"You shall not covet your neighbor's wife; and you shall not desire your neighbor's house, his field, his male servant, his female servant, his ox, his donkey, or anything that is your neighbor's."* If what you're looking at causes you to covet (lust after or desire what someone else has), stop looking at it. If you're wanting or desiring someone's body, spouse, job, or house, it's time to take a break.

Proverbs 4:23a (NLT) says, *"Guard your heart above all else."* In this verse, the word *heart* is not only referring to your heart, but also your *mind*. We are to guard it carefully, alert to make sure it isn't harmed.

God knows the destructiveness of coveting and wants to help us live an abundant life in Him. So follow His lead when He asks you to take necessary steps in guarding your mind.

WHAT WE READ

I'm sure you don't have to be told this to know it's true, but the Lord wants to remind us He cares about what we're reading. I can get pretty caught up in people's stories. You too? And the Internet has figured out the algorithms to offer lots of opportunities for me to be distracted.

When I read about a murder, I want to know the ins and outs, and the whys and hows. Joel calls it the tragic story of the day. He's come home many times when I'm anxious to share a tragic story with him. Are they edifying and lifegiving? No. Do they produce peace in my mind? No. So why do I spend so much time giving them my attention?

What about the latest news with all the disunity going on in the world? Or the hate being spewed out all over the place? I think it's good to be aware of current events and know what's going on in the world so that we know how to pray. But if what we're reading is causing us to get angry, or fear, or stress us out, we probably need to cool it with how much we're reading.

God sees it all. We can find peace because He knows everything going on and He's not freaking out. So neither should we. If what we are reading is causing our hearts to give way to fear, or our minds to wander into unhealthy places, then it's time to change our reading habits.

God is calling you and me up higher. He wants our focus to shift from the things around us to the things above us (heaven).

We live in a very distracting world, and its standards continue to move further away from God's Word, and closer to the acceptance of all things. We aren't called to complacency but rather, holiness. Live in a way that honors God, including what you listen to, what you watch, and what you read.

We are all a work in progress, so don't get discouraged if you feel like you're failing at living for the Lord. God's mercies are new every morning. Today is a great day to posture your heart in a place of humility before God and surrender everything to Him. Let's pray together, for the Lord to have His way in our lives:

Heavenly Father,

We come before You and repent for putting our desires before Yours. We ask You to forgive us for being complacent and justifying sin. Please give us a greater level of wisdom and discernment. Help us to love what You love and hate what You hate. We want to be more like You, living in a way that points others to Your beauty. We pray the things we listen to, watch, and read would be pleasing to You. We love You and know You have our best in mind!

In Your name we pray, amen.

Chapter 15

Life is Worth Fighting For

"I have fought the good fight, I have finished the race, I have kept the faith."
2 Timothy 4:7 (NIV)

This week Jael (my 10-year-old daughter) and I decorated the house for Christmas! I thought this year I would decorate by myself while the kids were at their Mimi's, but Jael asked if she could stay to help.

Because she knows me so well, she knew how to persuade me by saying we could watch a Hallmark movie together when our work was done. I couldn't turn down the opportunity to create a lifelong memory with her, so of course I let her stay!

We turned on Christmas music. She made hot cocoa. And we worked together to make our house full of holiday cheer! When we finished, we picked out a Christmas movie. I opened a bottle of sparkling cider and busted out the ice cream. We snuggled up together in Christmas blankets and enjoyed the predictable, but oh so sweet and cozy movie.

As she laid in my arms, I had the following thoughts: "What if I had given up? What if I had lost my fight to live and allowed sorrow to overwhelm me? I would have missed out on this precious time with my daughter." It was a sobering moment. In a way it felt holy, realizing life is worth the fight for moments like the one I was living in.

I don't feel my best (yet), but I'm still here. I get to watch my children grow and create memories with them that will affect their lives forever.

I was talking with a friend on the phone the other day who recently witnessed her momma's last breath on earth. She shared some of the grieving process during our conversation, and something she said impacted me greatly. She talked about the power of her mom's *presence*.

Even though her mom required care near the end of her life, and much of her time was spent lying on the couch, her mom's presence was what she wanted. Being able to call and hear her voice, knowing she was still there, was enough. Her mom didn't have to do anything to be needed and loved.

Now that her mother is in heaven, there's a void in my friend's life. Her mom fought to live a beautiful, godly life. And each day she did was a gift to her family.

WHEN FIGHTING LOOKS DIFFERENT

The days I spent lying down over many months, were still a gift to my children. I fought to be present, even if it looked a little different than what you might think fighting means. My presence was needed.

Talking to my friend made me realize even more how the enemy has lied to me. He's tried to convince me I'm not doing enough. That I'm not being the mom or wife my family needs. That I'm not worth the money we've spent on doctors. And that everyone would be better off without me. But I've fought to recognize these are lies. My presence is enough. And yours is too.

Had I given up, I would have missed on so much life. Getting to kiss Gracie's little cheeks and sing "Jesus Loves Me" to her before bed each night. Watching Harvey carry out an epic trick play at his flag football game and score a touchdown. Helping Jael create a first-place hat that won the title of *wackiest* at school. Buying Harvey a toilet plunger and tying it to his head for his wacky hat idea.

Things like taking Esther on a date to pick out a toy, then enjoying a Chick-Fil-A lunch together, just the two of us. Watching Joel build a chicken mansion (it's a chicken coop, but it's the biggest I've ever seen). Painting said coop yellow as a family then scrubbing the paint off the kid's bodies. Going on a girls' road trip with Jael to spend time with friends in South Dakota. Being there to hold Grace when she wasn't feeling well and hearing her say, "I want you, Mommy!" Soaking up the snuggles we both needed. Singing Esther her song (a song I wrote just for her) each night. Hearing, "You're the best mom in the world," from Harvey every day. Walking around our property with Joel while watching Esther play with our chickens, realizing the dreams we dreamt together are coming to pass.

Had I given up the fight too soon, I would not have known my sister as a foster parent. It has been such a joy to watch her as a mother. I would never have known my foster nieces or heard about the miraculous ways God brought them to Hannah. I would have never seen her prayers answered or witnessed her beaming with love for the children in her arms.

Many wonderful and priceless memories have been made in the last two to three years. This season has been marked by tears, but it's also been marked by beauty. And while I haven't felt like myself, it doesn't mean life is no longer beautiful.

We aren't promised an easy life. We'll no doubt go through seasons we'd prefer to fast forward, the same way we skip over a boring scene in a movie. But obviously, life doesn't work that way.

So, instead of wishing for the next season to come, let's learn to find value in the *now*. Let's ask the Lord why He allows the waiting, why He entrusts us with the pain.

APPRECIATING EACH SEASON

Winter is my least favorite season. Once Christmas is over, I want the cold and snow to go away. I can't wait for spring to come. But the older I get, the more I recognize and appreciate the beauty each season brings. I decided I can simply view winter as dark and cold. Or I can change my perspective and remember it's cozy and less chaotic too.

This season of my life has felt like a really long winter—like I've been hibernating—but I've been fighting to see and understand the good coming from it. I'm determined to not give up. I have a lot to look forward to, and so do you! Don't forget that spring is on its way!

We are in this race together, so let's run it with the intention of winning. I love 1 Corinthians 9:24–27 (NIV) which says, *"Do you not know that in a race all the runners run, but only one gets the prize? Run in such a way as to get the prize. Everyone who competes in the games goes into strict training. They do it to get a crown that will not last, but we do it to get a crown that will last forever. There-fore I do not run like someone running aimlessly; I do not fight like a boxer beating the air. No, I strike a blow to my body and make it my slave so that after I have preached to others, I myself will not be disqualified for the prize."*

There is purpose in us running this race of life well! We can look forward to a heavenly reward and leave a stunning legacy when we live for Jesus here on earth.

I want 2 Timothy 4:7 (NIV) to be said of me, *"I have fought the good fight, I have finished the race, I have kept the faith."* Life is worth the fight. It's worth contending for. Many times I've thought and said, "All I want is to feel normal again." But until I do, I will put in the work of choosing to hope, of trusting the Lord no matter what, of making memories, and of being present for my family and others. I will work to put Jesus first and run my race well, because it's worth it.

At times, Philippians 4:13 (NKJV) feels easier to quote than to live out: *"I can do all things through Christ who strengthens me."* But the longer I'm on this health journey, the more I realize how true this verse is. I can and am fighting my way through this winter season and finding beauty in it.

Each morning, I'm choosing joy instead of sorrow. I'm focusing on the blessings in my life and being present for my children, like wiping Gracie's tears after she gets a boo-boo, and putting a "bangaid" (band aid) on her wounds. I'm reading Esther a book and reminding her of how strong and beautiful she is. I am playing checkers with Harvey and telling him what an awesome husband and father he will be. I'm teaching Jael how to cook and reminding her of her worth in Jesus. I am making dinners for Joel and praying for him daily. I'm falling asleep with my hand on his arm each night, hoping he knows how in-love I am. And I am looking for ways to encourage strangers everywhere I go.

Even if this was it, even if I never preached another sermon or led another worship song, these simple blessings would make life worth fighting for! I feel the sweetness of the gift of life right now as I write, the tenderness of this moment.

Life is but a vapor, friend. We're not promised tomorrow. So let's live each day intentionally loving those around us, focusing on the good instead of everything that's going wrong.

I can still do many things. I've been discouraged for a while because I don't feel normal doing them yet. But my perspective is changing as I become more thankful no matter how I feel.

For a long time, I couldn't look at photos from before I got sick without feeling such a sense of grief. I longed for what once was. Prior to getting ill I was strong and capable, and the pictures reflected health, joy, and adventure! Now, every photo since July 27th, 2019 comes with different emotions. I might have been smiling in them, but I remember how I felt. I remember the pain, the fear, and the longing to be whole again. Maybe you know exactly what I'm talking about because you have experienced life prior to and post whatever trial you've had to walk through.

But the longer this goes on, I realize I don't have to let grief ruin a good photo. Instead, I can be thankful for *all* the blessings I've experienced in life. I can recognize this season for what it is... *a season.* And remember, seasons change.

Today, I'm more grateful for the strength being built in me now, while continuing to expect total healing. It's been quite the journey, with lots of ups and downs, but I'm not quitting. And be encouraged not to give up either. We will make it through this time of suffering.

I've said it many times in this book because I want so badly for you to never quit. Please, don't give up! You can do this. You might not know what is next, but God does. The power of the Most High God is living inside of you. Joy is coming! You will laugh again. The best is not behind you, but rather in front of you. So friend, hold on to the rope of hope because this too shall pass. You are here for such a time as this (Esther 4:14). So don't let the enemy try to convince you that your life holds no purpose, and the world would be better off without you. Those are lies. You are valued and needed right now, no matter how messy your life might be.

IS THIS YOU?

I feel like the Lord just gave me a picture of someone on their couch, weeping. With tears pouring down their face, they are saying, "I can't. I can't do this anymore." But God wants to speak directly to your heart right now and tell you that you *can* and you *will*!

I hear Him declaring *courage* over you because there is hope for your future! This book was written for you, from someone still in the trial. It's to you—one who is in a trial too. Together, we are going to make it through the fire and through the storm. We're going to recognize the strength of the Lord, and that His power really is made perfect in our weakness. And even though the main cry of our heart is to feel normal again, I know without a doubt He is with us, that He loves us, and that one day we will testify of His miracle-working power in our life. It's coming!

So let's agree to not give up, my friend. Like you, I know the feelings of hopelessness and despair. I understand what it is to fear for your future. But I also know hope and joy in the midst of pain, and I'm seeing the beauty of life, no matter the season. I'm praying you will too.

THE GOLDEN TICKET

Have you ever been crying out to God for something and someone else gets what you've been praying for? Perhaps you've been longing to be married, and you just got news of your friend's engagement. Maybe like me, you've been asking God to heal you, and you learn of someone else who was just miraculously healed. Maybe you've been longing to have a baby, struggling to get pregnant, and your Instagram feed announces that someone is expecting. Or perhaps it's been a season of financial stress, and someone you know just got their dream job and is *making bank* while doing what they love.

This morning as I worshiped in church, I could hear the kindness of my Savior speaking to me. He told me that someone else's miracle won't take away from mine. It's not like the golden ticket in *Willy Wonka and the Chocolate Factory* where only one person can receive it. When someone else's prayers are answered, let it be a reminder God hears the cries of our hearts and is still in the miracle-working business.

The enemy would like to use someone else's breakthrough to try and convince us God heard their prayer but has forgotten ours. That's simply not the truth. Instead, let the miracles around you build up faith for your own. If God can do it for them, He can do it for you and me.

I'm not gonna lie. At times I've felt a tinge of sadness when I've heard about another's miracle because I'm still waiting for mine. But I recognize that in those moments, the enemy of my soul is trying to steal my faith and hope. He's trying to make me feel like I've been forgotten. But friends, we need to hear stories of the miraculous. Why? Because it builds up our faith for what's coming.

The truth is that God's timing for your prayer to be answered might be different from those around you. But His timing is perfect. I picture Him giving every one of you a golden ticket. The dates for when they can be used are different, but every person has access to one.

Someone else's miracle won't take away from mine.

You number my wanderings;
Put my tears in Your bottle;
Are they not in Your book?
When I cry out to You, then my enemies will turn back;
This I know, because God is for me.
In God (I will praise His word),
In the Lord (I will praise His word),
In God I have put my trust...
Psalm 56:8-11a (NKJV)

Chapter 16

No Matter What and Even If

*"But even if he doesn't, we want to make it clear to you,
Your Majesty, that we will never serve your gods or wor-
ship the gold statue you have set up."*
Daniel 3:18 (NLT)

You might be asking, "What about those who have cried out for a miracle, standing in faith, but they didn't receive their miracle this side of heaven?" I've had to process this question because I've asked it too. It's been in the back of my mind the last couple of years. I've seen people of faith consistently declaring the goodness of God, believing for His touch on their lives, pass away. Why didn't they receive a miracle, and what if I don't experience one either? I think it's worth talking about, so let's go there together.

I don't have the answer to the question asking why some people get miraculously healed on earth, while others receive their healing when they take their first breath in heaven. But I do know this... God is good, and He is faithful all of the time. I know He wants us to continue to trust Him no matter what. Hebrews 11:6 (MSG) says, *"It's impossible to please God apart from faith.*

And why? Because anyone who wants to approach God must believe both that he exists and that he cares enough to respond to those who seek him."

We will not understand some things on earth, but God offers us peace that passes all understanding (Philippians 4:7) when we don't. When things don't make sense, God's looking for our heart's response to be trust. We're to trust Him *even if*, and *no matter what*. He sees the end from the beginning. And even when it doesn't feel true, He still works everything out for good.

I would rather spend my entire life believing for a miracle, declaring my trust in God, and living with joyful anticipation of good things to come (hope), than doubt His faithfulness when things aren't going my way.

When we read about the heroes of the faith in Hebrews 11, verse 13 (NLT) states, *"All these people died still believing what God had promised them. They did not receive what was promised, but they saw it all from a distance and welcomed it. They agreed that they were foreigners and nomads here on earth."* I like how the NIV starts this verse, *"All these people were still living by faith when they died."* I want this said of me. That no matter what happens here on earth, I remain confident in the goodness of God.

We might not see the promise fulfilled here on earth. But like the heroes of the faith, we can live knowing the fulfillment is coming and live for something greater than ourselves. Their choices made a difference in the generations to come, you and I are reaping the benefits of their faith. Their obedience to God—their *yes* to Him—helped pave the way for His blessings in our lives.

And friend, when you say *yes* to God with faith over fear, it will affect your children, grandchildren, and generations to follow.

When we aren't seeing the promise fulfilled, it doesn't mean that we should ever stop believing. It doesn't mean God is less faithful. Sometimes the answer to our prayer will be fulfilled in time to come, as was the case with the heroes of the faith. Let's learn from their example and respond the same way they did. These men and women knew that what God promised was going to happen, and they are listed in the Bible because they spent their entire lives believing it. Their faith never wavered when they didn't see the promises fulfilled. Why? Because they lived knowing that in the right time, in God's timing, He would bring it to pass.

With that said, remember it's okay to ask God questions. It's okay to ask God *why*. David was a man after God's heart and he often came before the Lord pouring out his soul, inquiring about his circumstances.

In Psalm 13:1-4 (NIV) David writes, *"How long, Lord? Will you forget me forever? How long will you hide your face from me? How long must I wrestle with my thoughts and day after day have sorrow in my heart? How long will my enemy triumph over me? Look on me and answer, Lord my God. Give light to my eyes, or I will sleep in death, and my enemy will say, 'I have overcome him,' and my foes will rejoice when I fall."*

David let God know what he was thinking and feeling, but he didn't stop there. He also acknowledged how he felt. And no matter what, David came back to trusting God, declaring truth despite his emotions. He chose to praise. For confirmation, look at how he ends this Psalm with verses 5-6 (NIV), "But I trust in your unfailing love; my heart rejoices in your salvation. I will sing the Lord's praise, for he has been good to me." This is a great template for us to use when we're in a trial.

First, draw close to the Lord. Secondly, be honest with Him. Then, choose to trust God and declare His truth. Lastly, remember to sing His praises. And no matter what, let this be your formula of walking out faith. God is good all the time, and all the time, God is good. Don't give up on believing! Don't quit your race. Your legacy will be blessed when you walk by faith.

I like to think about who I would have been during Bible times. Would I have been listed in the Hall of Faith? Would I have died having spent my entire life believing? I sure hope so! But the awesome thing is I'm here now, for such a time as this, and I get to learn from the heroes. I get to choose to live as they did. So, I'm choosing to believe, to fight the good fight, and declare the goodness of God no matter what. I'm choosing to trust I will continue to see His faithfulness and miracle-working power in my life until I take my last breath on earth, and my first in heaven.

No matter what happens on this earth, we can live with hope, walk in peace, experience joy, and receive the strength we need to run our race well. So instead of going through life fearful, let's work on declaring *even if* and *no matter what* kind of faith. That means if you're prone to say, "What if my situation never changes and things don't get better" change it up. Instead, start saying, "*Even if* my situation doesn't change, You will take care of me, God. And *no matter what*, I know You are faithful."

For me, this looks like saying, "*Even if* I never feel normal again (although I will in Jesus' name!), You will give me strength to get through each day. And *no matter what* I face, You love me and are for me."

Even If = Faith

What If = Fear

Even if and *no matter what*, God is good. The enemy wants us to focus on all that could go wrong in our lives. But God wants us to believe for all that could go right! Starting today, choose to place your trust in the Lord, *even if* and *no matter what*.

WHY ME?

When going through a trial, it's natural to ask, "Why me?" I've asked it many times in this season, and I realize there are many people who have been put in situations that would cause them to ask the same. Many people from the Bible in fact.

ESTHER

Esther could have asked this question when she lost both of her parents and was raised by her cousin. She could have asked, "Why me?" when taken from her home and all she knew. She could have kicked and screamed along the way, "Why God, why me?"

God knew the end from the beginning. He chose her to do something mighty for the kingdom. He chose her to be a voice for her people and help rescue a nation from death. *Why her?* Because God had a plan, and He would use all the hardship she went through for her good and His glory.

MOSES

Moses could have asked this question when he learned about his heritage. Why did he have to grow up separated from his family? Why did he struggle to speak? God knew the end from the beginning. He placed Moses in the Egyptian household for a purpose greater than he or his family knew at the time. But God knew one day Moses would help lead the Israelites out of bondage and into freedom. He knew one day Moses would declare, "Let my people go!" *Why him?* Because God chose to use someone with an unexpected beginning to bring about a legacy of freedom!

JOSEPH

Joseph could have asked this question when his brothers threw him into a pit and sold him into slavery simply because he was favored. He could have asked, "Why me?" when he was wrongly accused then sent to prison. He could have spent his years in captivity accusing God of injustice, questioning His faithfulness, and losing hope in the dreams God had given to him. But God knew the end from the beginning.

Though it took years of waiting, Joseph's betrayal and imprisonment was a set up for his good and God's glory! Joseph did not give up. He was a mouthpiece for the Lord and God called him to be a beacon of restoration and forgiveness. *Why Joseph?* Because He knew Joseph would remain faithful to Him and inspire generations to come of what trusting the Lord and walking in forgiveness can do.

PAUL AND SILAS

Paul and Silas could have asked this question after being beaten and thrown into prison for delivering a demon possessed girl. They could have gone to the Lord in misery and said, "We are preaching and healing in Your name, and this is how we are to be treated?" But instead, they opened their mouths in worship.

God knew the end from the beginning. He knew that their bondage would bring about others' freedom; that the situation meant to harm them would be used for their good and God's glory. *Why Paul and Silas?* Because God knew this part of their story would encourage multitudes of people (myself included) to praise through the trial instead of complaining through the pain.

JESUS

He could have asked this question too. King Jesus, the perfect, spotless Lamb of God. He could have said, "Father, why me? I've done no wrong." He endured suffering, accusation, and death. God knew the end from the beginning. He knew death would not be final. Jesus didn't question God's plan but instead surrendered to it. He trusted that God would use it all for good and His glory! *Why Jesus?* Because we all desperately need a Savior!

Those who inspire us, live remarkably. They press on in the face of adversity and cling to the promises of God. I'm thankful for each one of the heroes of the faith—both those mentioned and those not. They are examples of trust and courage, and resilience and hope. I'm grateful their response to hardship was to press on in faith instead of giving in to despair. Why? Because they remind me God knows the end from the beginning of my own journey. And they encourage me to trust God through it.

The heroes we look to for inspiration would not be named so if they hadn't gone through a time of testing. I've heard it said your test becomes your testimony. What if these heroes had given up? What if they had allowed their trials to harden their hearts and turn away from God? We would not be looking to them for inspiration today had their hardships robbed them of their trust in God.

The truth is that no one *wants* to go through trials. No one wants to suffer. As mentioned before, we live in a fallen world. And because of that fact, hardship is inevitable. But with the hardship comes an opportunity to rise up in faith and show the world where true hope comes from. You see, if life is but a vapor, then suffering is too. Our time on earth is precious, for with it comes the chance to live out what we believe.

Think about it. Is God good all the time, or is He not? Does God work all things out for good, or does He not? Does God see the end from the beginning and allow hardship because He has a greater purpose, or not? Is He trustworthy, or not? I say that He is. That He is good all the time and works all things for good. That He can be trusted, and His plan can be too, *no matter what.*

> But I will sing of Your power;
> Yes, I will sing aloud of Your mercy in the morning;
> For you have been my defense
> And a refuge in the day of my trouble.
> To You, O my Strength, I will sing praises;
> For God is my defense,
> My God of mercy.
> **Psalm 59:16–17 (NKJV)**

Chapter 17

You Can Be a Hero

*When you're going through a trial, kindness is
never taken for granted. Help becomes a lifeline.
And the helper, a hero.*

I've thought about the many people who have helped me on my journey to health. Every kindness shown and selfless service along the way has been a gift. I'd call them acts of heroism—people coming to my rescue. And it got me thinking that we all can be heroes. It doesn't take a cape and the ability to fly. It just takes a willingness to love others by truly seeing them, being aware of their needs, and having a heart to serve.

I want to spend a little time sharing specific heroes in my life, along with their heroic acts. It's not because they expected recognition, but because they are worth mentioning. I hope their acts of kindness inspire you to be a hero in a loved one's, a neighbor's, or even a stranger's life.

MY MOM

I've already shared about her, but I have to mention mom here too. She displayed selflessness and generosity by making sure I had turkey soup every day for five weeks. I needed something nutritious to eat and something my stomach could handle, and she ensured it. She stayed awake in the night to pray over me, and she rubbed my legs for hours to bring me a little relief. Those were moments of genuine love and selflessness. There's so much more she's done for me through this trial. I could never thank her enough. She's a true hero, laying her life down to care for another.

MY SISTER, HANNAH

She became like a second momma to my Gracie girl, getting up in the night to feed her. She loved her like her own. Hannah drove to my house twice a week to take care of me and the kids. She ran errands for us, drove my children to their activities, and was always willing to listen to me process. I've expressed how I felt physically and emotionally to Hannah more than anyone else. I never wanted to wear people out by talking about the symptoms, but with Hannah I felt safe to share everything. That has truly been a gift to me. She came to my rescue so many times.

She has not only cared for me heroically, but now she's a hero in the lives of her foster children, living selflessly every day to love others well. She's not married yet, but that hasn't stopped her from living out what she's called to do. Let her inspire those of you who are waiting. You have a purpose whether you're single or wed. God wants to use you right now, right where you're at, and right in the season you're in.

MY MOTHER-IN-LOVE

Every time she watched my children, she gave me a chance to rest. There were many texts she sent me with a prayer or encouraging word. She surprised me with thoughtful gifts to uplift and bless me—timely ones that have meant so much. She's been there not only for me, but for my children and Joel as well.

MY FRIEND, AMANDA

One time she came over unannounced with dinner for my family. I heard the knock on the door and opened it to find her beautiful face. She wasn't deterred by the tissues in my nose from being sick, but rather, she gave me a hug and let me know she was praying. She always offered to take my kids whenever I needed help. It's a gift to have a friend like her, someone who loves you when you're at your best, but even more in your time of need.

MY FRIEND, STEFFANI

There was one point in this journey that felt incredibly heavy, and I just wanted it to be over. I was struggling to fight and felt like giving up. Before I knew it, my dear friend Steffani was at my door with flowers and popcorn in hand. She and her husband had come to pray. My response? Tears. And thankfulness. She and Dave laid hands on me and declared the attack of the enemy to stop in Jesus' name. I remember Dave praying, "Satan, get your hands off her now!" He was commanding the attack of the enemy to stop! I sensed the power and presence of God and knew them coming was heaven ordained.

Steffani and I text frequently, and she has prayed for me all throughout this journey. She had never just shown up at my house like she did that night. But because she was sensitive to the Holy Spirit, she knew it was just what I needed.

Something I learned from Steffani that feels very heroic is to follow up with people. For example, if you prayed for a friend's appointment, send a text asking how it went. Find out how someone's sick child you were praying for is doing now. She's taught me how to better care for people and the details of their lives. When you take the time to see how someone is doing, it demonstrates you care for them, and it means more than you probably realize.

MY FRIEND, CHRESA

Joel and I spent our ten-year anniversary at my parent's house. Yep, that's right. It was during the time when I was very ill and staying with my folks, so Joel spent the night there with me. Instead of our planned getaway to Hawaii, we slept in my mom and dad's bed, and spent the next day at their house. My lifelong friend, Chresa, brought us an anniversary dinner from Cracker Barrel (she and I worked there together many years ago), and a couple of games to play too. It was so incredibly thoughtful and a bright spot in our day. I'll never forget how she took the time to bless us that day. She knew we couldn't go out, so she made it special for us while we were stuck in.

MY FRIEND, HEATHER

She asked if I needed help getting Easter baskets for my kids. This was also during the time I was staying at my parent's house, so I took her up on her offer. She drove to the store, took pictures of basket ideas, and delivered them out to me. She also brought us meals and offered many times to help in any way she could.

MY FRIEND GROUP

I'm not sure what I would've done without my friend group: Emily, Harmony, Leslie, and Amanda. Emily drove me to appointments.

Harmony came to my house and prayed over me, as well as called me on the days I needed it most. Leslie sent Spirit-led texts of encouragement. And I already mentioned Amanda. These ladies have seen me at my worst. They've walked with me through everything and haven't given up believing for my healing. They've stood by my side as I've ugly cried and have helped instill hope in me for my future, reminding me this will come to an end.

MY FRIEND, TONI

She has given up social media for years, fasting it for my healing. That blows me away! She hasn't stopped standing in faith for my miracle. She's someone I've been able to share the good, the bad, and the ugly with. She's a thoughtful gift-giver, asking the Lord what to give and when to give it. She has prayed so much for me over the years, checking in every week to see how I am. I can never thank her enough.

AUNT JAN

One day when I felt very down, I received a card in the mail from my Aunt Jan. Her words encouraged me in the battle. It was exactly what I needed to remind me that God was fighting for me. Her continual prayers and encouragement have been a gift.

MY PRAYER WARRIORS

To those who lift me up in prayer every day, what a gift. Warriors like Tammie and Bob, Miss Linda, Pastor John, and many others, have blessed me and I am overwhelmed by their love and support. I know God has heard every prayer and their faith has caught His attention.

PASTORS JOHN AND MISS LINDA

I had a month of setbacks over two years into this journey and felt like I was on the brink of a nervous breakdown. I had trouble sleeping again, endured a headache every day for almost that entire month, and had increased nerve pain. Setbacks can be very discouraging, and I was desperate for help.

A friend of mine encouraged me to reach out to the elders of the church and ask for prayer, so I contacted my former pastors, John and Miss Linda. They responded quickly and days later came to my house to pray over me.

Pastor John read James 5:14–16 (NKJV) which says, *"Is anyone among you sick? Let him call for the elders of the church, and let them pray over him, anointing him with oil in the name of the Lord. And the prayer of faith will save the sick, and the Lord will raise him up. And if he has committed sins, he will be forgiven. Confess your trespasses to one another, and pray for one another, that you may be healed. The effective, fervent prayer of a righteous man avails much."* He pointed out how biblical it was to ask them to come and pray for me. They anointed my head with oil, laid hands on me, and declared my body healed.

The tears spilled as Pastor John reminded me of the joy I walked in when he hired me to work at the church so many years ago. "Carefree Kaitlyn, the girl I've missed so much." Both Pastor John and Miss Linda are believing for my total healing, awaiting the day I'm symptom-free and abounding in joy once more!

It's hard to explain how precious a time it was to have them in my home, and to hear them declare God's goodness and faithfulness. They did not have to come. But I'm beyond thankful that they did. Thank you, pastors, for taking the time to minister to me. Thank you for your wisdom and continued prayers. Two days after Pastor John and Miss Linda prayed for me, the headache I'd had for so long was gone. Praise God!

PASTOR BRIAN

One day when I was on Facebook, I was drawn to a powerful re-demption story that one of my friends had shared. The story led me to the page of a pastor named Brian. As I scrolled through his profile, I saw that God had used him to help bring physical heal-ing to people, many being healed while he prayed for them on the phone. So, I sent him a message and asked if he'd be willing to pray for *me*. To my surprise and encouragement, he responded quickly and said he would be happy to call and pray.

We set up a time to talk, and he spent one and a half hours ministering to me. He sought the Lord on my behalf. He listened, and he prayed.

He spoke to me about the importance of my heart being healthy, and that if there was any area of unforgiveness in me, to choose that day to forgive. He was kind. I knew he cared, not be-cause I went to his church (he doesn't even know me and we live in different states), but because He loves God and has a heart for His children. This man didn't have to take the time to talk with me, but I'm so glad that he did. Through our conversation the Lord showed me a few things that made a difference in the health of my heart.

In 3 John 1:2 (NKJV) it says, *"Beloved, I pray that you may prosper in all things and be in health, just as your soul prospers."* God doesn't just want me healthy physically, He wants me healthy spiritually and emotionally too. The same is true for you. Pastor Brian knew this, and as he followed the Lord's leading, he helped me to see where my heart needed healing.

I think I'll share what God showed me through that conversation another time, in another book perhaps. But what I will say about it is that my heart needed to release some things. What I thought was going to be a short prayer for healing physically, turned into a long conversation that led to some deep heart work. I needed that. Thank you, Pastor. The care you showed me impacted my life greatly, and I'm forever thankful.

If you're in a difficult season, you might not have the capacity to reach out to others the way you'd like to. When I was at my sickest, I could not be as thoughtful as I once was. I didn't have the energy to be creative with gifts or plan get-togethers like I had before. I found myself on the receiving end more than the giving end.

It is true that it's more blessed to give than to receive (Acts 20:35). I felt agony in not being able to give like I used to, but guess what? My capacity is growing again. I'm not back to where I used to be, but little by little, I'm doing more. I'm able to throw a party here and there, spend more time on gifts, and care for others a little more. With the changing of seasons often comes a change in capacity.

In the days and weeks after each of my children was born, my house was a disaster. My capacity to keep it picked up and clean changed because my precious pumpkins were taking all of my attention. But the floors eventually got swept and the laundry put away. No one remembers the house being messy. What my children will remember, however, is that I took the time to be with them. They will recall me playing like I was a mother cat with her kittens, or that I was the *pretend* mom and they were my *pretend* kids. I've always thought it was hilarious when they asked me to pretend to be their mom.

One of the most important things I've learned in the last couple of years is that it's ok to say *no*. And often, it's necessary, even to things you want to do. It's been over two and a half years since I've led worship in a main service, and I want to lead again. But I'm giving my body the time it needs to heal. I want to hike mountains with my mountain-conquering friend (ahem, Emily!), but I have to say no until I feel better. I want to take care of those in need. To be a hero for others. There are many things I want to do, but until God gives me the green light, I'm going to stay in this season of rest. And that's okay.

When you're going through a trial, kindness is never taken for granted. Help becomes a lifeline. The helper a hero.

You can be a hero with a simple act of thoughtfulness. If you look for an opportunity to bless someone, you'll find it. There are many people who are hurting right now. Many who are struggling to provide, searching for hope, and experiencing pain. You could be the answer to their prayer—the hero in their story.

Maybe send a card with an encouraging word. Make a meal for a mom who is sick. Offer to watch someone's kids for the day. Send a text declaring God's truth over their situation. Pick up the phone and taking the time to talk. Give a meaningful gift to remind them God's not finished with them yet.

MY ENCOURAGERS

On many days, I've asked God for a reminder of His love for me, or a sign confirming I will be healed. And almost every time I've prayed for those specific things, God has used someone to answer those prayers.

Sometimes the answer has looked like dear Dana sending me a text saying she's trusting God for my healing and knows it's coming. Or my friend Angie sending me a wall hanging that says... *Blessed is she who believed that the Lord would fulfill His promise to her.* (Luke 1:45 NIV) Angie has prayed diligently for my healing. Thank you, friend.

On my last day of work, a precious lady from the women's ministry I pastored handed me an envelope. She said God woke her up that morning and told her to give me what was inside. The contents paid for what I was about to pursue next medically. It was a gift that went beyond financial blessing because it was a reminder to me that God would continue to provide, and that it didn't depend on my work.

My friend Joy sent a necklace and note of encouragement about having strength like King David before he became king. I wear it and am reminded of the power that's within me! Joy has listened to me process, she's seen me weep, and has lifted my arms in prayer!

My Aunt Dena sent me a text asking me to meet with her because she had a prophetic gift for me. She took the time to get a word from the Lord, then found gifts to represent each aspect of the word. I have part of the gift sitting on my kitchen counter and am reminded of God's goodness when I see it. When I wear the necklace from Aunt Dena that says *Revived* on it, I cling to God's promise that He is the One who revives me, and my faith for it to come to pass is strengthened.

Another dear friend sent me a check and said it was from God. What she didn't know was I had to pay one of the largest out-of-pocket bills of this entire season *that* week. Her generous heart and obedience to the Lord showed me once again that God has and will continue to take care of me.

My precious friend Allie has checked on me all throughout this journey. She's been a source of encouragement simply by letting me know she's thinking of me and that I've not been forgotten. This year on my birthday she brought over the most wonderful welcome sign for my house. It has a chicken on it! We sat on my porch swing and caught up on life. I love you, Allie.

So many others have reached out, consistently prayed for my healing and have stood in faith for my miracle.

Michelle is a new friend made through this season of difficulty. She had to resign from her job due to health conditions too. We connected via mutual friends over Instagram, exchanged numbers and have become dear friends. Michelle needs a miracle too, so if you pray for me, please also include her in your prayers!

My sister found a sign that says "This Too Shall Pass." She gave it to me to be reminded of its message. I placed it in my living room where I can see it every day. My mom found a different sign with the same powerful words, and it's in my kitchen where I can see it daily and be encouraged.

Tammy, Katie, and Brian at Natural Health Center of the Rockies have been a consistent source of encouragement and blessing to me. Through their generosity, I've been reminded of God's provision in my life, and that He will meet all my needs. Their kindness has been an answer to prayer, and I can't thank them enough for how they've shown me care.

I'm sure I've missed people who have been a source of encouragement and hope to me the past few years. And if I did, forgive me for not mentioning you by name. Please know, however, that every text, card, and prayer have blessed me beyond measure.

Goodness! I am surrounded by people who love well, those who look for opportunities to bless others, and who are directed by the Lord as to what to do, what to say, and the timing of when it's most needed. I can't tell you how many times I've had a very difficult day and received multiple texts from people saying I'm on their heart and they are praying for me. That might seem like a simple and easy thing to do, but it has meant the world to me. It's revealed that God has not forgotten about me, and I'm on His heart too! He uses us to remind others of His goodness, faithfulness, and love! He uses others to remind us He is the God who sees.

GOD SEES

I've heard about the various names of God. They are all so powerful. There is Jehovah Rapha (the Lord who heals). Jehovah Nissi (the Lord my banner). Jehovah Jireh (God will provide). Jehovah Shalom (the Lord is peace). Jehovah Shammah (the Lord is there/present). But one I haven't heard often and was reminded of this week is El Roi (the God who sees me).

It's been on my mind the last couple of days. El Roi, the God who sees not just me, but you and everything going on in this world. When someone reaches out to me with a prayer or word of encouragement, it's a reminder that God sees my situation. He hasn't turned His eyes away from me. Truly, I'm always so encouraged when people reach out saying they are praying, because it shows I'm on God's heart, that He sees and hasn't forgotten.

My dad is a wise man. He reminded me of something Corrie Ten Boom said. "There is no pit so deep that God's love is not deeper still." He pointed out how not everyone is surrounded by family and friends the way I am. But everyone has access to the same God who cares, who loves, and who sees.

If you do not have family and friends to lift you up in your battle, even still, you are not alone. *"Even when I walk through the darkest valley, I will not be afraid, for you are close beside me. Your rod and your staff protect and comfort me."* (Psalm 23:4 NLT) He is with you. And it's Him who will strengthen and comfort you.

Let the examples of those who have shown *me* care be motivation for you to step out, reach out, and embrace someone in need in a way you've never done before.

You can be confident God has not turned a blind eye to abuse, sickness, or suffering. He sees, and He is working, even when it doesn't feel that way. You might feel overlooked or forgotten. Maybe you've been wronged, and you wonder if things will ever be made right. Today, take comfort in knowing God has seen it all. He sees you now. And He is the Lord who heals. He is the Lord your banner. And He is the Lord your peace.

God is faithful and He is good. Trials come, but so do victories. Winter seasons are hard, but spring is next. El Roi, the God who sees you, is not finished working on your behalf.

Chapter 18

What Happens Next?

"Let us hold fast the confession of our hope without
wavering, for He who promised is faithful."
Hebrews 10:23 (NKJV)

I'm not entirely sure what will happen next. I recently met with my twenty-fifth medical practitioner, a specialist in Denver who went over the MRI I had a few months back and brought some more clarity to it. He explained I have a disruption in my jugular vein. The issue is not in my neck, but rather my skull. And he'd like me to have an echocardiogram because there's a heart condition consistent with my symptoms. So, I'll get the echo, have the follow-up appointment, and see what needs to be done next.

But guess what? I'm still believing for a miracle!

I'll continue to hold on to the rope of hope. I will contend for my healing and the healing of others. I'll continue to write, sing the new songs God is giving me, and believe there is purpose in the waiting. I will continue to get out of bed each morning and declare my body whole. I'll look for the good in each day and thank God for His faithfulness every night. I'll remind my soul of who I am and Whose I am. I'll remember that my time on earth is temporary, which means the pain is too.

It would be nice to know the end date to this season. When you're pregnant, it's endurable because you know after nine months of being uncomfortable, you'll give birth, and the discomfort will end. But when you're struggling with your health, you don't really know when you'll get better. That can make the waiting period feel daunting at times. However, if God told me I'd feel normal again one year from today, it wouldn't require the same level of trust, faith, and hope I'm being challenged to live in and therefore strengthened to walk in, now. I've received a similar word from a few people, telling me there is an end date to all of this. And every time I remind myself of it, I feel hope increasing.

This will come to an end, but until it does, I will try to learn all God is wanting to teach me in this season!

I love 2 Corinthians 1:3–4 (NKJV) which says, *"Blessed be the God and Father of our Lord Jesus Christ, the Father of mercies and God of all comfort, who comforts us in all our tribulation, that we may be able to comfort those who are in any trouble, with the comfort with which we ourselves are comforted by God."* God is comforting me, and in return I'm able to comfort others better because of it.

He's caring for me through those around me. 2 Corinthians 7:6 (NKJV) says, *"Nevertheless God, who comforts the downcast, comforted us by the coming of Titus."* You can be God's comfort to someone today. Isn't that amazing?

God uses everything for good. He really does. Even though I still struggle daily and desperately want to feel good again, I see how God is strengthening me. And now, I understand the source of true joy and hope.

I will contend for my miracle and your miracle too. I won't stop believing.

There will be miracles!

I want to live, making known the goodness of God! On the harder days, I often sense the enemy of my soul trying to get me down. It seems he is trying to persuade me to give in to sorrow. But I don't want him to get any glory from my story. So on those days, I take a deep breath and remind myself of the promises of God! When I choose joy in the midst of pain, or trust in my Heavenly Father when things don't make sense, I'm declaring the power of God is overcoming Satan's attempt to ruin my life. In that victory, I am strengthened!

Remember, we are in a fight. And it's not with flesh and blood, but rather with the powers of darkness—spiritual forces that want to destroy you and me (Ephesians 6:12). When the enemy attacks, don't just take it. Instead, fight back and use the Armor of God (like we talked about in chapter 6).

I don't want the enemy to get any glory from my story.

My desire is to be known for joy, even while in this health struggle. I want my family and I to shine the light of Jesus, spreading His love and hope. I want to bless the heart of my Savior in worship, and I want to serve others as best I can. The healthier I get, the bigger my capacity to do God's work will be. So I also want to continue having grace on my body and rest when necessary, knowing I'll be able to do more eventually.

I want to continue looking for beauty, whether it be in the sunrise, in my children's laughter, in realizing the gift of watching my children grow, or in going to bed beside my husband each night. No matter what, I am blessed. I've been given a beautiful life. This trial has tried to taint it. It has tried to smear the beauty with its sorrow, but the pain won't win in the end. This I know.

The pain won't win in the end!

YOU ARE ENOUGH

As I wait for my next steps towards healing, there are many moments filled with hope. But in keeping it real with you, there are also many moments of sorrow. I've battled some sadness the past few days. I try really hard to hold on to hope, to walk in joy, and declare truth despite how I feel. But some days, I just need to acknowledge the discouragement and be ok with admitting I'm struggling. I'm walking this journey out in the strength of the Lord, but sometimes I get tired along the way and need to grieve what feels lost in this season. It's been a few of those days recently.

Towards the end of today, Joel and I talked, and I let the tears spill as I poured out the thoughts running through my head this week. *I wish I didn't need to rest so much. I long to lead worship again. I miss dancing. I want to feel capable. I want to hike mountains. I want my balance back. I want the pain to go away.* I let the tears fall while Joel looked me in the eyes and said, "You are enough." (Cue more tears.)

He has told me that I'm doing enough, I'm doing a great job, I'm beautiful, and he is glad to be married to me. But he's never said those exact words before—*you are enough*. I took a bath shortly after we talked, and as I let what he said take root in my heart, truly believing he spoke the truth, I felt peace.

I don't have to do anything more to be loved, wanted, and needed. The same is true for you. *You are enough.* Joel looking at me and assuring me he's not leaving and that I am enough, was just what I needed to hear. I believe our Heavenly Father wants you to know the same thing too. *You are enough.* So while we may not know what is coming next, we can be certain our worth is settled and rest in that truth.

THE GRIEVING PROCESS

Part of my ability to move forward has required that I allow myself to grieve. I could try to shove the sorrow away, not dealing with the emotions that come with it. But the healthier thing to do is to make space for my feelings, be honest with the Lord about them, and allow Him to walk me through the grief I've felt from this season.

I've actually felt a greater level of peace by recognizing my need to grieve. I told my sister Hannah recently that I lament pretty much every day. I hadn't realized it until I began to process my feelings, but it's true. Almost every day, I'm faced with a moment of grief where I wish I felt normal, or pain-free and like myself again. But the more I acknowledge sorrow for what it is, and that it's a part of life, the quicker I move on to an attitude of thankfulness for all my blessings.

We can't ignore pain. We can't shove grief away and pretend it isn't there. We need to let ourselves cry, knowing just because we're grieving doesn't mean we're not also giving thanks or believing for better things to come. Even Jesus wept (John 11:35). He allowed Himself to grieve when he heard about the death of His friend Lazarus.

Think about that. Jesus knew a miracle was about to take place, but still took a moment to feel the sadness of what had happened. That amazes me. I picture Jesus at the tomb where Lazarus was laid, knowing He had just been weeping and groaning from within, and it causes me to wonder if His cheeks were still stained with tears as He called for his friend to come forth!

I have wept many times in this season, tears streaming from the pain of it all. But at the same time, I have confessed my trust in God, my Healer, and have stood in faith for my body to be made whole. Seeing Jesus respond to sorrow in a similar way gives me such peace to know you can weep over something while at the same time believing for it to get better! Perhaps tears still fell as Jesus said the following three things:

"Did I not say to you that if you would believe you would see the glory of God?" (John 11:40b NKJV)

"Father, I thank You that You have heard Me. And I know that You always hear Me, but because of the people who are standing by I said this, that they may believe that You sent Me." (John 11:41b–42 NKJV)

"Lazarus, come forth!" (John 11:43b NKJV)

I can hear Him saying it all with great passion. It moves me deeply knowing that my Savior wept, but at the same time commanded a dead man to rise. Jesus grieved, but He didn't let it consume Him. I feel there are those of you who need to allow yourself to grieve—to know it's ok to weep over what's painful. Over hope that has been deferred or over circumstances that have brought sorrow. Like Jesus, it's okay to let yourself cry over that which has been lost. But also like Jesus, grief doesn't have to consume you.

Remember there is a time to weep, a time to laugh, a time to mourn, and a time to dance (Ecclesiastes 3:4). I pray you allow yourself to feel the sorrow if you need to, but at the same time believe God will work all things out for good.

You can weep over something and believe
for it to get better at the same time!

As I sat in church this morning, I thought about Jesus on the cross when He cried out, *"'Eli, Eli, lama sabachthani?' that is, 'My God, My God, why have You forsaken Me?'"* (Matthew 27:46 NKJV) In His time of agony, Jesus cried out to His Father, questioning His presence.

Did Jesus not fully trust God? Of course He did, but He suffered tremendously. And just before He yielded up His Spirit,

He took a moment to make known the separation He felt from God. Perhaps it was due to Him taking on the weight of the world's sin and feeling the distance between Him and His Father because of it. But I also wonder if the excruciating physical pain Jesus endured on the cross caused a moment of feeling abandoned by God.

I'm so thankful knowing Jesus can relate to my pain, and the questions I've had about my heavenly Father because of it. *God, where are you? Have you forgotten about me? Why are you allowing this?* But what Jesus did next reveals His continued trust in God: He yielded up His spirit. You can have it all, God! All I am, is Yours. I surrender. Your will be done.

Jesus experienced the greatest suffering of all mankind and lived His entire life from first breath to what the world thought was His final one, yielded to His Father's will. In my moments of questioning God's heart towards me, I can remember Jesus on the cross. He had a similar moment. And He knew His Father had a redemptive plan. The most glorious resurrection was about to take place. Death was about to be defeated! God knows what's coming next for you and me as well. And it's good, my friend, because His plans for us are good.

I continue thinking about the woman with the issue of blood, and how she had enough hope left in her after twelve years of suffering to pursue her healing. What if she had just accepted her condition and fell for the lie saying it would never change? Like her, I know one encounter with Jesus will cause everything that's wrong in my body to be made right. In that hope I live.

As we sang, "Yeshua, I love You," in church this morning, I had more thoughts about the woman with the issue of blood. *What did she do after she was healed? What did her life look like after having suffered for twelve years to being healed in an instant?* I pictured her praising Jesus, thanking Him for the miracle that took place in her body. Singing the same words I sang this morning,

"Yeshua, I love you!" I pictured her going to sleep with a smile on her face, finally free from pain. I felt like I was supposed to imagine myself the moment I am healed too—to picture what it will be like once I am well. I don't want to lose sight of being able to see the promise! And I believe a powerful exercise of faith is to see myself well before I am.

I mentioned earlier that I've gained thirty-seven pounds since I was at my lowest weight. I'm thankful to be looking healthier. Because I look better, people would never know all my body goes through every day, and that's a good thing. Not everyone needs to know how wacky I feel.

The grocery clerk doesn't need to know if I feel like I'm bouncing up and down as they bag up my food. They just need to see the light of Jesus shining through me. I feel purpose in my life when I push through discomfort and offer hope to others.

When I take time to encourage a stranger or deliver a meal to someone in need, I find great joy. It doesn't involve me organizing an event or leading worship at church like I used to do, but giving a neighbor some of our farm-fresh eggs, baking a loaf of sourdough bread for my sister, or sending a gift to a friend in need helps me move forward. These things matter too. My assignment is different in this season, but no less beautiful.

The value of my life is not based on the number of people I impact, but by my obedience to the Lord and the way I love Him and everyone I cross paths with. The same is true for you. You don't have to be an Instagram influencer or be well known in order to be valuable and have purpose on earth. Just love those around you well! And now that I am feeling stronger, I want to encourage others however He leads.

LEGACY

I think about legacy often. *What will be said of me when I enter glory? What will my children remember about me and talk about the most?* My hope is that I'll be known for joy and being someone who had a steady faith in Jesus through all of life's ups and downs.

Even when I was unsure about what was next, I want people to say I stood for truth and walked in love. I want it said that I was bold, but humble. I want my kids to say I was FUN! Most importantly, I want my life to have shined the love and light of Jesus, always pointing people to Him. I want it said of me that I was a woman who lived with hope, not defined by my circumstances, and I daily chose joy. I want those closest to me, especially my husband and children, to be able to say I loved them well. I want to be known as someone who was genuine in all they did.

I will try to live this way on the days I feel good, and on the days I spend in bed. Because the way I choose to walk through this battle will impact not only me, but also my husband, children, and those watching and listening to my story unfold.

I want to encourage you to think about your legacy too. Spend time on this, asking God for direction. And then live in a way that shapes the legacy you want to leave.

I know life can be very difficult, and perhaps my trial pales in comparison to the one you're walking through right now. You might feel the world is against you, as if nothing ever seems to go your way. What tough season have you been walking in? Maybe your marriage is over, and your heart is torn in pieces. Perhaps you lost a child and are wondering how you could ever move forward and feel joy again. I feel like there are those of you reading this who are struggling financially and are tired of working so hard to make ends meet. You've been crying out to God for breakthrough, hoping one day you won't feel the pressure of financial stress. Listen to me, friends... you are not alone.

There is hope, and you have not been forgotten. Life can be incredibly difficult and painful, but in the midst of hardship, God is working. I know this because I've been in that season and experiencing beauty at the same time. So don't give up. More of your story will be written, pages filled with the good things to come. You may not know what comes next, but Your heavenly Father most certainly does.

FINDING NEW PURPOSE

This question often arises in our minds when going through a trial. *What is the purpose of life?* The longer I'm on this journey to health, the more I understand that God created us to be in relationship with Him. He loves us beyond measure. And because we live in a fallen world, there will be hardship. But through it, God wants us to draw closer to Him.

As cliché as it may sound, our purpose is to know Him and to make Him known. To live each day making the most of every opportunity (Ephesians 5:16) and finding all the reasons we have to give thanks. I've said it before, and I'll say it again: we are not guaranteed an easy life. In fact, we are told we will have trials and sorrow (John 16:33), but we can take heart because Jesus over-comes the world. We get to walk out our faith, choose joy when it would be easier to give in to sorrow, walk in hope when others would despair, and love when so many people are full of hate. We get to shine the light of Jesus to a world that desperately needs Him!

You are needed to help others find new purpose after hardships. The light inside of you is needed in a world that's full of darkness. The enemy is on the prowl, seeking to devour (1 Peter 5:8), wanting to take us out before our time. Let's not give into him or his lies because God has a better way. Let's choose life, my friend, and help others choose it too. Together, let's declare today we will live and not die! And as you take the next step towards full healing, command the voice of the enemy to be silenced in your life.

Our purpose is to know Him and to make Him known.

Here's what I've come to realize. God is the only One who fully knows what I go through every day. He knows my every thought, every fear, all the discomfort I feel, the way I choose joy, and my fight to hold on to hope. He sees every tear. He hears every prayer. He alone is with me every second of this journey. This realization is precious to me.

The fact that only Jesus knows all I endure, no matter how hard I might try to explain my symptoms and worries to others, brings comfort. Really, it's only Jesus who fully comprehends. In that truth, I see beauty. I have an intimacy with my Savior that I'll never have with anyone else.

At times I want those closest to me to understand the depth of what I feel on a daily basis. Why? Because we share what's important with those we love. And in some ways, when I feel like others know what I'm enduring, then I'm not alone in it. But having the revelation God knows every single symptom I have and every thought that runs through my head, gives me so much peace. I don't have to let others know the ups and downs throughout my day. God knows, and He is with me through it all.

God is with you too. He will never leave your side. He is for you and hasn't forgotten about you. Every tear you've cried, He's seen. Every prayer you've uttered, He's heard. He is faithful and good and will come through for you. Your life might not look the way you imagined and hoped, but He is working on your behalf and beauty is coming.

We are going to make it. Let's shine brightly and remind the world that Jesus is alive and at work in us!

LIVE IN TRUTH

My daughter Grace, only two years old, walked around today proudly declaring over and over again, "I look beautiful! I look beautiful! I look beautiful!" And as she did, I felt an impact on my heart.

She was in her pajamas, unbathed with messy hair, but full of confidence in who she was. She has heard us repeatedly tell her, "Gracie, you're beautiful and we love you." And she lives in that truth, no matter what she looks like. If only we would live this way too, listening to the truths our Father is speaking over us and living in them no matter what.

For me, this means declaring I am healed despite how I feel. For you it might mean believing you are loved even though you've felt abandoned. Or professing you're blessed when you don't know how you're going to pay your bills. Like Gracie, live in the truth your Father has spoken over you, no matter what you or your circumstances look like.

WON'T STOP BELIEVING

It's been 892 days... seventy-three since I began writing about this journey. I don't know how many more days I will be asking God for healing, but friends, I'll never stop believing for it. Through all the highs and lows in each day, I will declare the faithfulness of God. I will not lose my laughter and I'll never stop looking for ways I can shine the light of Jesus.

Let's not forget this: God allows trials, but He uses them for good. I've learned so much in the last two and half years. My understanding of the Word has grown. My compassion for those suffering has increased. My ability to choose joy has been strengthened. My faith for the miraculous has been secured. My thankfulness for all that is beautiful in this life has expanded. And my hope for what's to come has been anchored in that which cannot be shaken. I am confident of this: I will see the goodness of the Lord in the land of the living (Psalm 27:13)!

Thank you for letting me share part of my story with you. I'm humbled and honored you took the time to read this book, and I pray that through it you were encouraged and strengthened. I pray you were built up in your faith and feel more hopeful for your tomorrows. Good things are coming, I really believe that!

THE INVITATION

If you read through this book having never received Jesus into your heart, and you feel the longing to do so, I'd love to lead you in a prayer of salvation.

God sent Jesus to earth as a baby, and He lived a sinless life here. As I shared all throughout this book, Jesus spent His life on earth healing the sick, loving the lost, and declaring the Good News of God. We are all sinners, but God is perfect. And so He wanted to make a way we could be close to Him, which is why He sent Jesus to us.

When Jesus died on the cross, He became the sacrifice for your sins and mine. He paid the ultimate price—a once and for all sacrifice. He took the weight of the world's sin and sickness on His body and declared IT IS FINISHED! His death brought us life. We are saved through His grace.

Three days after His death on the cross, He rose again, declaring death had no hold on Him! And for those who are saved, death has no hold on them either. The Bible says if you declare with your mouth that Jesus is Lord and believe in your heart God raised Him from the dead, you will be saved (Romans 10:9). Your eternity is secured, and you enter into a life of hope like you could not have without Jesus. He is the answer to all the world's problems. He is the One we need. So, if you want to invite Him into your heart right now, declare this with your mouth and believe it in your heart.

Dear Jesus,

You are what's been missing from my life all along. I need You, and I'm inviting You into my heart today. I'm asking You to become the Lord of my life. Thank You for forgiving me. Help me to live my life with You and for You from this day forward. Thank You for loving me, and for saving me through Your death on the cross. Thank You for rising up from the grave and showing me that nothing is impossible for You. I give You my life today.

In Your name I pray, amen.

If you prayed this prayer, welcome to the family of God! Heaven is rejoicing!

What a joy it is to be a part of the family of God, to know Him and to make Him known.

With so much love and joyfully His,
~Kaitlyn

A Closing Prayer

I believe in the power of prayer, so I'd like to close this book praying for everyone who needs Jesus' touch on their lives. For those waiting on the Lord for breakthrough. As you read the words of this cry from my heart for you, know that God is listening, and His faithfulness will never fail you.

Heavenly Father,

I thank You for loving us so well. You see every need. Not one tear is lost on You. You care about the details of our lives. I'm asking You for miracles right now. For those reading who need a mighty touch in their bodies, oh Jesus, heal them now, I pray!

For those who feel hopeless and want to give up, I pray You would infuse them with Your power and love right now. That there would be a turnaround in their trial! I speak life over them, life and not death, in Jesus' name!

I lift up those who have struggled to get pregnant. Father, I'm asking You to bless their womb right now! I pray the desires of their heart would be met.

For those who have lost a child or loved one, Father I pray Your comfort would wash over them. Heal hearts and release Your joy.

And for those who work so hard but can't seem to make ends meet, God, You are Jehovah Jireh, the great Provider. I ask You for overflow right now! I pray for divine connections and supernatural finances to come through quickly in Your name.

For those who long to be married, God I ask for the right spouse to come quickly. Do what only You can do! Fulfill dreams, I pray. I'm asking You to do the miraculous!

I believe!

In Your precious and powerful name I pray, amen!

"And let us not grow weary while doing good, for in due season we shall reap if we do not lose heart."
Galatians 6:9 (NKJV)

Scriptures to Declare and Cling To

"I would have lost heart, unless I had believed that I would see the goodness of the LORD in the land of the living."

Psalm 27:13 (NKJV)

"And we know that all things work together for good to those who love God, to those who are the called according to His purpose."

Romans 8:28 (NKJV)

"Being confident of this very thing, that He who has begun a good work in you will complete it until the day of Jesus Christ."

Philippians 1:6 (NKJV)

"Yet in all these things we are more than conquerors through Him who loved us."

Romans 8:37 (NKJV)

"But if the spirit of Him who raised Jesus from the dead dwells in you, He who raised Christ from the dead will also give life to your mortal bodies through His Spirit who dwells in you."

Romans 8:11 (NKJV)

"For God has not given us a spirit of fear, but of power and of love and of a sound mind."

2 Timothy 1:7 (NKJV)

"Fear not, for I am with you; be not dismayed, for I am your God. I will strengthen you, yes, I will help you, I will uphold you with My righteous right hand."

Isaiah 41:10 (NKJV)

"My flesh and my heart fail; but God is the strength of my heart and my portion forever."

Psalm 73:26 (NKJV)

"Do not sorrow, for the joy of the LORD is your strength."

Nehemiah 8:10b (NKJV)

"He gives power to the weak, and to those who have no might He increases strength. Even the youths shall faint and be weary, and the young men shall utterly fall, but those who wait on the LORD shall renew their strength; they shall mount up on wings like eagles, they shall run and not be weary, they shall walk and not faint."

Isaiah 40:29–31 (NKJV)

Notes

Chapter 1:
Footnote from Luke 5 taken from Tyndale's Life Application Study Bible NKJV Life Application Study Bible. Copyright © 1988, 1989, 1990, 1991, 1993, 1996 by Tyndale House Publishers, Inc., Carol Stream, IL 60188. All rights reserved.

Chapter 2:
To read the full article about the biodome experiment, visit naturalawakenings.com. "Strong Winds Strong Roots: What Trees Teach Us About Life" by Dennis Merrit.

Chapter 7:
Footnote from Luke 8 taken from Tyndale's Life Application Study Bible NKJV Life Application Study Bible. Copyright © 1988, 1989, 1990, 1991, 1993, 1996 by Tyndale House Publishers, Inc., Carol Stream, IL 60188. All rights reserved.

Chapter 8:
Petruzzello, Melissa. "Playing with Wildfire: 5 Amazing Adaptations of Pyrophytic Plants". Encyclopedia Britannica, Invalid Date, https://www.britannica.com/list/5-amazing-adaptations-of-pyrophytic-plants. Accessed 17 February 2022.

About the Author

Life can throw some crazy, painful curveballs, but with Jesus by your side it's possible to endure everything that comes your way with peace and joy. No matter what you're going through, what dream you are waiting to see unfold, you are not alone. There is hope. Immanuel, God with us, is by your side. El Roi, The God who sees, is watching you. Heaven is cheering you on and I am too! I want to come alongside you and share what I've been learning during a very difficult health battle. Despite daily discomfort and pain for years, I feel the strength of the Lord, and believe He wants me to share with you what He's taught me through this journey, so you will also be strengthened.

I would love to know if this book ministered to you in any way. If it has, or if you would like to follow along with my health journey, please reach out via Instagram @kaitlyn_c_scott, Facebook @kaitlyncscott, or email me at 2kaitlynscott@gmail.com. You can also connect with me at kaitlyncscott.com.

~Kaitlyn

Kaitlyn, her husband Joel, and their four amazing children live in the beautiful state of Colorado. They enjoy their country home which includes a dozen chickens, a rabbit, a cat, and a gecko. They love spending time in the great outdoors hiking and fishing together. As a family, they pray for miracles every day, knowing the goodness and power of God is very much alive! They love Jesus and want the world to know He loves them too.